WRITER to WRITER

BODIE & BROCK THOENE

BETHANY HOUSE PUBLISHERS
MINNEAPOLIS, MINNESOTA 55438

Published by Bethany House Publishers
A Ministry of Bethany Fellowship, Inc.
6820 Auto Club Road, Minneapolis, Minnesota 55438

Printed in the United States of America

Library of Congress Cataloging-in-Publication Data

Thoene, Bodie, 1951–
    Writer to writer / Bodie and Brock Thoene.
       p. cm.

    I. Authorship. I. Thoene, Brock, 1952–   II. Title.
PN147.T364   1990
808'.02—dc20   90–492
ISBN 1–55661–042–4   CIP

To Carol Johnson . . .

of course.

Books by Brock and Bodie Thoene

The Zion Covenant

Vienna Prelude
Prague Counterpoint
Munich Signature
Jerusalem Interlude
Danzig Passage
Warsaw Requiem

The Zion Chronicles

The Gates of Zion
A Daughter of Zion
The Return to Zion
A Light in Zion
The Key to Zion

Saga of the Sierras

The Man From Shadow Ridge
Riders of the Silver Rim
Gold Rush Prodigal
Sequoia Scout

Non-Fiction

Protecting Your Income and Your Family's Future
Writer to Writer

Contents

Introduction: Beginnings 9
1. So You Wanna Be a Writer?................... 13
2. "Commit Your Way . . ." 21
3. Starting Small................................. 33
4. Help Along the Way 39
5. The Writer's Market 49
6. What Are Your Interests?...................... 59
7. W, W, W, W, W, and H....................... 67
8. Turkey Carcass Writing........................ 75
9. Pick One and Write! 81
10. Clip Clippings, Not Coupons.................. 87
11. Making a Perfect Match....................... 95
12. Me (Query) Contact an Editor (Query) 107
13. Don't Be a Deadbeat! 119
14. Interviewing Unmasked........................ 127
15. Loving a Many-Slanted Thing.................. 135
16. Editing Till It Hurts............................ 141
17. Dressing for Success........................... 149
18. Practically Perfect Book Proposals.............. 157
19. Thoene and Thoene............................ 163
Appendix 169
    The Professional Free-lancer's Checklist
    Contacting an Editor With a Story Idea
    Tips to Remember When Contacting an Editor

BODIE THOENE was described by John Wayne as "a writer with talent that captures the people and the times!" She is best known as author of *The Fall Guy*. She worked for John Wayne's Batjac Productions and ABC Circle Films as a writer and researcher. Her research on *The Zion Chronicles* included in-depth interviews with those who lived through the events portrayed in these novels. She and her husband Brock make a home for their children on a ranch in California.

BROCK THOENE has often been described by Bodie as "an essential half of this writing team." With degrees in both history and education, Brock has, in his role of researcher and story-line consultant, added the vital dimension of historical accuracy to the creative process. He is the author of the nonfiction volume titled, *Protecting Your Income and Your Family's Future.*

Beginnings . . .

*I*s it possible that the course of a child's life can be set as early as the third grade? As a successful writer looking back on all the things that have happened over the years, nothing is as significant as that morning in May when Mama took us all to Sunday school at our neighborhood Methodist church.

The room reserved for Children's Church was packed with kids from grades three through six. I sat in a small chair near the front where a tall, grim-faced, bean-pole of a woman led the songs. I was having difficulty learning to read, so I could not read the words in the songbook, but I moved my mouth and hummed the melody.

Suddenly the teacher must have noticed that my lips were moving like a badly dubbed Japanese movie. In indignation she singled me out and demanded that I read the words of the song aloud. When I could not, she ridiculed me in front of the other kids, and I left the crowded room in tears.

I could hear the piano and the singing as I ran down the hall and then down the steps that led to the basement. There I waited out the hour until Mama would come to take me home. And there I vowed that I would never return to that Sunday school room—no matter what!

The basement was dark and pleasantly cool. Neat rows

of folding chairs were stacked along the cinder-block walls, and over in the corner, covered by a tarp, was an extra altar from the social hall.

A small wooden cross poked out from beneath the tarp, and for some reason I was drawn to that visual sign of God's love, even though it would be many years before I understood its meaning. Somehow I felt as though I needed to tell God that I was sorry. So very sorry that I was not good enough to join the other kids singing in Sunday school!

I could still hear distant happy voices as I knelt before that covered altar. None of my family had yet come to the understanding that being a Christian is more than going to church. We did not realize that knowing the Lord and accepting His forgiveness were the keys to new life. But Mama sometimes took us kids to church, and we had a *respect* for God and for doing right. I was quite certain that God existed and was so afraid of speaking His name in vain (whatever that meant) that I refrained from using His name at all!

It was on those terms that I knelt before Him. "You, up there . . . ," I whispered, feeling as if I had truly come into a holy presence, "I am Bodie. Mama said I should be in Sunday school, but I ran away and I'm sorry. I can't read the songs. Mrs. White made fun of me. I don't want to go back unless I can read." I paused for a long time. I wanted God to think about this for a while. Surely He would understand, I thought. "I want to read like the other kids more than anything. Honest. If only you would help me learn to read good, I would do anything you want. I would go back into Mrs. White's class even. I would read the words from the songbook out loud. I would . . . maybe if you want I would even write something just for you and read it out loud."

That was the bargain I made with God. It was a bargain

I forgot for many, many years. But He heard me that morning as I hid in humiliation. He heard the desire of my heart. And in the dark basement of St. Marks He began to answer . . .

*S*erve wholeheartedly, as if you were serving the Lord, not men.

Ephesians 6:7

*N*othing goes by luck in composition. . . . The best you can write will be the best you are.

Thoreau

*T*he pen is a formidable weapon, but a man can kill himself with it a great deal more easily then he can other people.

George Dennison Prentice

So You Wanna Be a Writer?

So you wanna be a writer?" Eddie Griffith chewed his cold cigar and looked at me as if I were something he wanted to step on.

"I *am* a writer," I said bravely, attempting to look much older than my sixteen years. "I want to write for your newspaper."

I thought I saw the fierce and terrible editor of my hometown newspaper almost smile at this remark. *Almost.*

"Is that so? Well, how old are you, kid?"

I squared my shoulders and lifted my chin, exuding self-confidence . . . I hoped.

"Old enough to write the kind of stuff the kids in this town will want to read. And not too old to turn them off with stuff they don't care about. I'm sixteen. How old are you?"

Mr. Griffith's eyes widened at my question. He hesitated a moment and then replied, "If I tell you, will you promise not to print it?" Now he was smiling in earnest, staring thoughtfully at his cigar. "So what have you got in mind, kid?" he asked. "Let's hear what you've got in mind."

For fifteen minutes he listened patiently as I laid out my grand plan to work as Editor-of-Student-Affairs for his paper. I would make weekly rounds of the local high schools and glean the best news from each. Interviews, sports events, opinions. The teen-age perspective would not only draw reader interest and foster community pride, it would also pull in advertising from stores geared to the youth market!

When I finally finished my spiel, Mr. Griffith crooked a finger at a man at a desk nearby. By now my hands were sweating with anticipation. Either this guy was the bouncer or Mr. Griffith was calling an on-the-spot consultation.

Griffith pointed at me with his cigar. "This kid says she's a writer," he growled. "Make her prove it, Berg. Stringer pay. Fifty cents an inch. One column a week in your section. Trial basis only. You got that, kid? One month to prove you're a writer."

I wanted to jump up and click my heels, but this was only the third time I'd worn high heels so I thought better of it.

"Eddie?" the man called Berg was begging, "What is this? You think I'm running a kindergarten over there? Eddie? *Please,* Eddie!"

As I look back over the years to that moment of my greatest triumph, I can still hear Eddie Griffith's sinister chuckle as Berg begged not to be stuck with such an assignment. I think now that two things delighted Eddie. One was getting me off his back, and the other was saddling his assistant with so much frustration. (Not until I thought about this years later did I recall—and recognize—the pained look on Berg's face. At the time, however, I was too young and too thrilled to care how my good fortune had come about.)

I hurried out of the office, pulled off my high heels,

14

and ran down the sidewalk to the nearest pay phone to call my mom.

"I got a job! With the *Californian*! Hey, Mom, *I'm a writer!*"

Somewhere in the midst of all my papers is a photocopy of my first paycheck. That first week I wrote twenty-four column inches, and my check was twelve dollars. I felt very rich. On the rare occasions when I've reread my earliest columns, I blush with embarrassment and marvel that those seasoned newspaper men not only allowed me to publish with them and shared their advice and years of experience with me but actually *paid* me for it!

Such a miracle has no logical explanation. It defies all reason, except that maybe the venerable old editor remembered something that I remember now as I tell you this story . . .

Everybody has to start somewhere!

Now it's my turn to ask, and your turn to answer the question: "So, you wanna be a writer?"

If your answer is *no,* put down this book. The material is top secret and guaranteed to demystify the mystery of publishing. Only hopeful writers are permitted to read this book.

If your answer is *yes,* then it is important to ask yourself a second question: Considering the hard work, emotional pain, disappointment, and stress of a writer's life, *why* do you want to be one?

Better look at this issue very closely. Either you're a self-abasing masochist who loves pain, or a glory-seeking egotist with delusions of grandeur . . . or just maybe God has put a desire in your heart to communicate with others through the written word.

Or maybe you think being a writer is something it is not. Maybe no one has told you this is a tough field to plant and an even tougher one to harvest. If that is the case (and it often is), no one will think less of you if you put this book down and leave it for someone else.

If I have learned anything since that afternoon when Eddie Griffith challenged me to *prove it,* it is this: Writing is always difficult and often disappointing. Self-doubt and questions about my own ability have floated to the surface a thousand times. Even Gold Medallion Awards and Book-of-the-Year plaques cannot quash such doubts.

"Are you kidding?" you say. "You feel uncertain sometimes? You feel as I do? Scared that maybe you're fooling yourself? That maybe you're doing the wrong thing?"

Since you asked, I'll tell you the truth. "You bet."

And it's at those moments that I must go back to the beginning. I don't mean back to that afternoon with Eddie Griffith and Berg. I mean the sort of beginning that requires a real look at the condition of my heart. After all, isn't that where all writers begin? With a heart's desire?

So I must go back and ask, "If writing is so difficult, then why do it?"

What's Your Motivation?

If you write in a journal or keep a diary, your style, form, and content are no one's business but your own. Writing for your own enjoyment requires sincerity, to be sure, but only enough attention to spelling and penmanship so that you can decipher your entries at a future date.

Writing for publication is another matter altogether. Even if writing remains an avocation rather than your full-time work, you will quickly discover that it is a craft, and a demanding one.

When making important decisions (and committing to study, polish, and practice your writing skills *is* an important decision), those who have Jesus at the center of their lives will find Him standing ready to offer counsel. Looking first to God's Word, then, is entirely appropriate.

Scriptural Principles Regarding Motivation

Ephesians 6:7 tells us to "serve wholeheartedly, as if you were serving the Lord, not men." This means that Christians, in whatever they do, must always see job performance and their witness to the world as inextricably linked.

Doesn't shoddy workmanship make you unhappy? How many times have you remarked "I'll never buy that brand again," or "I just won't patronize that organization" because the quality of the product or service was mediocre or substandard?

In the same way that poor quality reflects on a manufacturer or a business, anything less than superior writing reflects on your Employer (if you're not certain who He is, go back and reread Eph. 6:7).

Christians cannot afford to be satisfied with anything second-rate. For too long we have made allowances for less than superior quality, comforting ourselves with the thought that if something was "done in a good cause," then a less stringent measure of performance could be applied. For this reason a world of unbelievers, whom we say we want to attract to Jesus, have come to associate Christianity with mediocrity.

Nowhere is this situation more critical than in publishing. Through print people are informed, challenged, entertained, uplifted, advised, cautioned, and inspired. High-quality writing grips readers' attention and leaves them satisfied that the message was intellectually, emotionally, and spiritually sound. Poor workmanship leaves readers with the impression that the subject matter must not be too important since the author has treated it so uncaringly.

Does this mean that you shouldn't become a writer unless you are perfect? Thankfully, no. If that were the case, only those with the highest E.Q.'s (ego quotients) would ever become writers! What I'm speaking of here is an attitude, a striving after perfection. If God is leading you to glorify Him through the written word, then He is also leading you to practice and polish.

Are You Spiritually Ready to Be a Writer?

Assuming that you're committed to serving wholeheartedly, what else must you consider? Here you should take to heart the words of Paul regarding the Corinthian believers. He says that they were "a letter from Christ, the result of our ministry, written not with ink but with the Spirit of the living God, not on tablets of stone but on tablets of human hearts" (2 Cor. 3:3).

Your life as a whole must reflect its Christ-centered nature. No other focus will serve. No values other than those of the Cross can remain at the core of your being, or that dichotomy will be apparent in your writing. Any desire for income, recognition, or popularity must be subordinate to your longing to be used by God to further His kingdom.

Does this mean that you should not expect to be paid for your efforts? Not at all. "The worker deserves his wages" (1 Tim. 5:18). Just remember that your primary motivation must be a desire to write as a means of service, keeping the letter from Christ written on your heart in the most visible and presentable condition.

Are You Practically Ready to Be a Writer?

If you can honestly say that your heart is centered on God and that you are willing to work hard to perfect your skills, then you are ready to consider writing. But a word of caution: No book can tell you how much writing God wants you to do and no book can do the hard, practical work for you.

This book is intended to provide you with a guide for improving your writing, a gentle introduction to the "secrets" of getting published, and a resource text for you to return to as God encourages you to expand your writing ministry. And you have a responsibility to act on the knowledge you gain. When a practice exercise is suggested, it is not simply an academic device. It is a practical step to publication. Use it! How's that for a challenge?

But this is much more than a textbook. It is a personal and practical discussion . . . just between us writers.

Writing for publication is a serious business. Not that it isn't fun or rewarding, because sometimes it's both . . . and sometimes it's neither!

*E*stablish the work of our hands for us—yes, establish the work of our hands.

Psalm 90:17

*I*f a book comes from the heart, it will continue to reach other hearts; all art and author-craft are of small amount to that.

Thomas Carlyle

Chapter: 2.

"Commit Your Way..."

*J*ack was a small middle-aged man with thinning hair and a weary smile. The kind of man who would sit quietly at a party and simply observe everyone else. He lived alone in a spacious ranch house in Beverly Hills. He was rich. He was talented. He was a successful screenwriter.

For years Jack had been a regular staff writer for the *Gunsmoke* series. He had been part of the team that adapted the *Sackett* novels of Louis L'Amour into a television mini-series starring Tom Selleck. (This was long before Selleck made it big in *Magnum P.I.*)

I was assigned to work with Jack and another writer on an ABC mini-series project. It was an enormous production, one that had priority over everything else in the hopper. Millions of dollars had been committed to portraying the life of a great man in a mini-series everyone thought would out rate *Roots*!

My task, as part of the writing team, was to provide the history, the facts, the legends, and the ideas that could come together to make "The Story." I loved every minute of the work.

Our home was a two-hour drive from the studio office on Wilshire Boulevard—if I was early enough to avoid the freeway rush hour. Often I would get up at four in the morning, be out the door by five and in my office at the stroke of seven. Surrounded by stacks of books and old news clippings and interview transcripts, I would be taking my first coffee break when everyone else was just beginning the day two hours later. My office was nicknamed "The War Room."

Every day more great material was excavated and passed on to Jack via hours of phone conversations or over long working lunches of pastrami sandwiches and cream sodas. While another writer slaved over a number of scenes we had discussed, Jack was quietly, earnestly working on others in the solitude of his home.

Months passed. The story was *right there*!

Jack complimented my work to studio heads and producers. He even offered me a contract to continue working with him after the ABC project was completed. I had never been so enthusiastic about anything I had worked on!

Deadline for the script was only three weeks away when I got a call from Jack. "Could you bring those tapes over? The ones from Stu? I want to hear how he talked again."

My husband, Brock, went with me to Jack's home. We knocked on the door of his studio and waited. Then Brock knocked again. Finally Jack appeared at the door. His sad eyes said much more than his smile and greeting. His skin was pale and waxy. He looked ill. Stepping aside, he asked us in.

The room we entered looked like the office of a great writer should look. Dark wood paneling. Bookshelves filled from floor to ceiling. Leather wingback chairs. Awards on the wall. Pictures of Jack with some great filmmakers. Jack with his mother. Jack with his brother.

And then there was the *desk*. Carved walnut. Huge. Impressive. Built in a horseshoe so he could be surrounded by work space. His big IBM typewriter sat in the center section, a stack of paper beside it. Sharpened pencils stood ready like little swords in a cup. I had never seen a neater, more organized desk. Everything was in place . . . ready to write!

Jack stood quietly, watching me scan his desk. A strange smile crept over his face.

Suddenly it hit me. The desk was *too* neat. And the paper beside the typewriter was *blank*!

"Are you finished?" I asked, afraid of his answer.

"Not quite," he said softly.

The truth was that Jack had not even begun to write.

All the months of work and research, story conferences and long hours . . . organizing . . . talking . . . discussing . . . reorganizing. What did any of it mean? All the great material in the world would not get the story written. Only Jack could do that. And Jack had not written. Not one word.

For some reason he had lost his confidence and discipline. Some terrible, unspoken *something* had cursed him with this neat desk and empty paper.

He knew that I knew, but neither of us mentioned it. We made small talk, and he asked us to stay for lunch. I pretended to have another appointment.

As we drove away, I said to Brock, "We're in trouble."

Some weeks later, after a half-finished script was submitted and rejected outright by the producers, Brock and I retreated to our mountain home, where we got snowed in for ten days. I continued to do my work by telephone.

One Friday night I spoke with Jack. He was making progress with the rewrite he said. He had finally pulled

23

himself together, and he wanted me to keep working with him on several big script projects he had lined up.

He did sound better. A little lighter than he had sounded for a while. I told him how much I was looking forward to working together for a long time to come. When we hung up I felt good. We had turned a corner. I hoped that Jack's desk was as messy as mine!

The next morning I got a phone call from our story editor. His voice was strained, and he asked me if I was sitting down. If Brock was nearby.

A wave of fear coursed through me. "What is it?" I asked.

"Bodie, Jack killed himself last night."

Jack had reasons for doing what he did. Reasons that made no sense to the rest of us, that saddened and angered us. Reasons that caused me to look closely at my own life and relationships with those around me.

Had I even talked to Jack about my faith in Christ?

Had I ever shared God's answer to his questions?

Had I really showed him God's love?

The answer to all of those questions was a sad "No."

This is a difficult story for me to tell even now. And you may wonder why I have chosen to relate it to you.

I have done so because there is a lesson in it for every writer.

Jack had everything any writer could imagine. Recognition by his peers. Money. Things. Future projects. But his life was empty. He had no purpose for what he was doing. Somewhere in his heart he knew that no one would remember his name unless they happened to catch the credits on a *Gunsmoke* rerun.

When Jack died, I suddenly realized that my life and work might be just as empty and meaningless. All the doors to my ambitions had opened up. I had contract offers, and agents and producers who were personal friends. I ate lunch every day in the Beverly Wilshire Hotel where all the beautiful people dined. My desk was full of work and accomplishments. But in reality—in the scope of eternity—my desk was just as empty as Jack's had been that day.

It hit me. "I might as well be digging a ditch in solitary confinement for all the impact my life and work are having on anyone!"

I did not want to end my life's work as a name in the credits of a television rerun!

As I looked around me, a light came on in my heart and I remembered the promise I had made to God when I was a child. He had fulfilled His part of the bargain, but what had I done? What was I *doing*?

"We finish our years as a tale that is told," wrote the psalmist. "The length of our days is seventy years—or eighty, if we have the strength; yet their span is but trouble and sorrow, for they quickly pass, and we fly away. . . . Teach us to number our days aright, that we may gain a heart of wisdom. . . . Establish the work of our hands for us—yes, establish the work of our hands" (Psalm 90:10, 12, 17).

How foolish are the goals we set for ourselves unless those goals are centered in Christ and look beyond the seventy years we are given on this earth! And yet, how great are even the smallest victories when our heart does battle for the King of Heaven!

For three more years I continued to work in the film industry. I still enjoyed it, but suddenly I began to see it only as a proving ground.

25

"Can you finish one hundred pages this week? Get it in on Friday? Doesn't have to be great. Just has to be finished." When challenges like that were issued, I asked God to help me meet deadlines *and* produce top-quality work. For the sake of reflecting the quality of Christ's craftsmanship, I prayed that I would be the best I could be.

Sometimes when I wrote I still thought I might as well have been digging a ditch, but I no longer felt alone in my effort. Jesus was right beside me, working with me. "This is the way. Walk in it."

Has God put the desire to write in your heart? Have you honestly analyzed your motives and the level of your commitment? If the answer to these questions is yes, then you should, in fact you *must,* write!

But wait a minute, you say. *I never made a bargain with God to become a writer. I've never traveled in foreign countries, or hobnobbed with famous people, or been recognized as an expert at anything! What can I possibly write about that anyone would want to read?*

Notice how cleverly Satan moves in to interfere with your desire to write when it becomes a desire to serve God? Almost the instant you decide that you want to follow God's leading into writing for publication, the devil is right there whispering in your ear that you'd be wasting your time.

Satan isn't called the father of lies for nothing, you know. He wants you to think you have nothing of value to offer because you haven't had unique experiences or training. Baloney! Listen to what Paul says in 1 Corinthians 12:8–11:

To one there is given through the Spirit the message

of wisdom, to another the message of knowledge by means of the same Spirit, to another faith by the same Spirit, to another gifts of healing by that one Spirit, to another miraculous powers, to another prophecy, to another distinguishing between spirits, to another speaking in different kinds of tongues, and to still another the interpretation of tongues. All these are the work of one and the same Spirit, and he gives them to each one, just as he determines.

See? You have a unique perspective! No one has the combination of gifts of the Spirit in the same proportion that you do. No one! What's more, God has been leading you through experiences and circumstances that contribute to you being you and no one else. No one has all your memories. Even identical twins have some experiences they haven't shared.

If God is calling you to be a writer, then He will lead you from this point on. And you will soon discover that He has known all along that you'd have this desire and has been building into your life a whole set of unique events from which you'll be able to draw your own one-of-a-kind perspective.

Most publications today can be called "special interest periodicals," meaning they appeal to a group of individuals with similar specific interests. People who read photography magazines are interested in learning more about taking pictures. Those who read parenting magazines are looking for answers to child-rearing questions. And so on. Special interest readers are seldom casual readers. They are either seriously investigating a particular sport, hobby, issue, or ministry, or they are already involved and are seeking to improve the quality of their involvement.

In other words, most readers are looking for answers.

From something as simple as increasing their knowledge of events and people to highly technical "how-to" studies, readers are people with questions. This puts the Christian writer in a perfect position to fulfill the command of Galatians 6:2: "Carry each other's burdens, and in this way you will fulfill the law of Christ."

Your contribution, your *ministry* if you will, may be to act as a channel through which information flows. You may not be the scientist who discovers a life-saving cure, but you might be exactly the one to communicate its discovery to others. You may not be able to offer expert advice or counsel, but if you can communicate clearly and effectively through the written word, you might very well be the source of immeasurable blessing by carrying someone else's counsel to those in need.

Do you think it's accidental that Jesus is called "the Word"? He appeared as the visible expression of God speaking to man. Remember what John said about Jesus in 1 John 1:1? "That which was from the beginning, which we have heard, which we have seen with our eyes, which we have looked at and our hands have touched—this we proclaim concerning the Word of life."

In what form was John's proclamation at that point? The *written* Word!

John did not claim to have caused the events of Jesus' life. He said he *proclaimed*.

Do you begin to see what a powerful, responsible position you are in if God has called you to write?

How Big Are the Possibilities

The 1989 edition of *Writer's Market* lists about 2,000 periodicals that accept unsolicited manuscripts. The number of such submissions accepted each year by these trade publications, consumer magazines, technical journals, and general interest periodicals ranges from a low of 10 to as high as 100. Taking an average figure of 25 per publication, a little quick multiplication tells us that 50,000 unsolicited articles will be published each year. That's 50,000 chances for free-lance writers (like you) to see their work appear in print.

You might be among the many who say at this point, "What has all this stuff got to do with me anyway? I want to write fiction! I want to write the story of my life! I don't want to write articles for a magazine or work on the staff of my local newspaper!"

Well, consider this: A free-lance article appearing in a large secular magazine may be read by half a million people. A novel, on the other hand, is considered a bestseller if it sells only 100,000 copies. You don't have to be a mathematical genius to figure out where your work gets the most exposure. And if your life and your work are dedicated to *proclaiming the Word,* such considerations are important.

Perhaps you feel that you are not important enough for anyone to want to read about your personal faith. If that is true, then ask yourself if you know any Christians who are doing great and wonderful things for the kingdom? Could you interview them? Write a story about them? Let them communicate through your written words?

What kind of human interest stories are right in your own backyard? Anything that might be of interest to a national publication? (Don't eliminate publications like the *National Enquirer* from your potential markets. Tabloids that dwell on sensationalism are read by more Americans than magazines like *U.S. News* or *Time.*) What we are talking about here is flooding the market with material that provides a different outlook than *I Met the Ghost of Elvis Hitchhiking to Memphis* . . .

Take a look through your local newspaper for possible stories. Can you find any women who, for the sake of Jesus, are caring for unwanted "crack" babies? How about some local Christian programs that care for the elderly in an unusual way? Or restaurant owners who donate extra food to a rescue mission?

A thousand stories out there are waiting for national attention. Stories about ordinary men and women who love the Lord and allow Him to direct their lives in ways that *change things.*

During the past few years the national press has feasted on the scandals in the lives of certain religious leaders. "So this is what Christianity is all about," they say.

Our answer as writers is simple: *"No. Christianity is about the carpenter from Nazareth. You see, He is still here . . . Helping the poor! Living through the life of this man or this woman! Let me tell you about the way He is working. . . ."*

And if *you* don't write it, who will? Or if someone else writes it, will he see it with your unique, God-given perspective? If God has called you to write, then you must think of the whole world as a field waiting to be sown with the seed of God's Word.

Miracles of love and hope are changing lives everywhere! You can play a vital part in proclaiming that good news!

*M*ake every effort to add to your faith goodness; and to goodness, knowledge . . . self-control . . . perseverance . . . godliness . . . brotherly kindness . . . love. For if you possess these qualities in *increasing* measure, they will keep you from being ineffective and unproductive in your knowledge of our Lord Jesus Christ.

2 Peter 1:5–8 (italics added)

*M*ost people don't realize that writing is a craft. You have to take your apprenticeship in it like anything else.

Katherine Anne Porter

A man may write at any time, if he will set himself doggedly to it.

Samuel Johnson

Starting Small

*R*edman was a tall, well-muscled two-year-old the first time we raced him at Bay Meadows Racetrack in San Francisco. Watching him run was a thrill. His powerful strides gobbled up the turf, and he crossed the finish line a full three lengths ahead of the second-place horse.

Redman was something special. A horse with heart as well as classic thoroughbred beauty. His copper-colored hide glistened with sweat as he was led, limping, into the winners' circle.

Redman had won his maiden race. He had set a record. But he had injured his right front leg doing it. The thrill of winning was completely forgotten as the vet announced that Redman would probably never race again. He had exerted himself far beyond what he could physically endure.

Redman had all the promise of a young horse capable of someday winning the Kentucky Derby, but after one race he was finished.

Things like that happen every day at the track. Horses are raced too young. Bones still soft and growing are stretched too far. Muscles are not mature enough to stand the strain. Great and promising young horses are crippled.

Our question was, *What now?* When a filly is injured, she can be returned to the farm as a brood mare. But what happens to a gelding who is incapable of breeding?

"Put him to sleep," said the vet.

"We'll take him home to the ranch," we replied. "Wait a while. Wait and see if time in the mountains might help him."

At that moment our sweet-tempered, magnificent Redman was worth about fifty cents a pound. Maybe less. We were teased unmercifully for wanting to take him home. *"You should call him Purina!"*

After three months of tender care the swelling went down, and we turned him loose with a herd of horses in a high, mountainous pasture. If he survived the winter and was forced to exercise his leg in the rough terrain, we reasoned, maybe he would be ridable again.

———

Every writer can learn something from the story of Redman. I cannot count the number of new, talented, and potentially *great* writers who have injured themselves in their race to publish. They choose the biggest and the best publishing houses in the country and send off unsolicited manuscripts. They put their heart into an envelope and mail it to a Junior Assistant Editor who returns it with a form letter stating that it "does not meet our present needs."

Finished articles by the hundreds are deposited on the slush piles of major New York magazines, only to be returned unread. Meanwhile, the writers hang out at their mailboxes. If the hope and energy of *waiting* for a positive reply could be measured, packaged, and sold as a vitamin, it would become a substitute for caffeine!

The pain of rejection is just as powerful and equally damaging. These early disappointments can cripple new writers, preventing them from ever running the race again, from ever pursuing what may be God's genuine call to *write!*

"Maybe I was wrong. Maybe God didn't really want me to be a writer."

"I was foolish to think I could ever do this and make it work."

"What was I thinking of? Nobody wants to read what I have to say."

Like Redman, they have run a twelve-furlong race when they should still have been in training!

If you feel like Redman—injured and hurting and out of the competition—read on. There is hope for you, and the promise that God will lead you to your goal—one step at a time. First of all, though, you have to be *willing* to take small steps. You have to lay aside your visions of winning the Kentucky Derby and return to training.

———

When I speak of "training," I am talking about learning to pace yourself.

If you have never published before, it does not make sense to make your first writing project a 700-page novel. Begin where you feel the most confident and comfortable and have the most experience.

If you have a definite opinion about something happening in the world or in your local community, why not write a letter to the Opinion Page of your local newspaper?

If your church needs help with the monthly newsletter, why not write a small piece for that publication?

Was your town heavily hit by a hurricane? Why not write an article for one of the tabloid magazines?

Like Redman, you may be setting yourself up for a serious injury if you write a short story for the *Ladies Home Journal* and then wait three months for a rejection letter.

It's okay to set your goals high. Just be certain that you aren't stretching too far too soon.

I have written for the top end of the publishing spectrum. I have also written for *Grit* and the *National Enquirer*. It's all part of training for the big race.

Keeping a Journal

One of the most valuable self-help devices you can adopt is a diary or journal. As with almost all endeavors, writing improves with practice and discipline. Making yourself sit down for a few minutes every single day to record your thoughts can be truly valuable. Journals are personal, not intended for publication or even critical review. Consequently you can be open and frank in your thoughts and unpretentious in your style.

Journals need not, in fact should not, be attempts at being highly intellectual. A journal is to be a reflection of your thoughts. You may record events of the day, conversations, chance encounters, and emotions. Initially the discipline of journal-keeping may produce what seem to be trivial reflections on mundane events, but stick with it! Soon you'll begin to notice that you have become comfortable with your journal; it feels natural, like confiding in a friend, and you have no difficulty selecting from the day's happenings exactly what it is you wish to record.

Journal-keeping has several practical benefits besides the enforced practice. The first is the stockpile of useful information you will collect for future writing efforts. For example, I write about particularly interesting people I meet, noting both their physical descriptions and patterns of speech. I also record descriptions of surroundings when I'm visiting new places.

Journal-keeping also gives a writer practice in brevity and clarity. Because journal entries are not meant to be 1,000-word essays, you must reduce what you want to record to its barest essentials. At the same time, if the thoughts you are recording are to be recoverable weeks, months, or even years in the future, your references cannot be too obscure or the meaning will be lost even to you, the author. Think of this aspect of journal-keeping as practice in being courteous to readers: No reader, however loyal or dedicated, will be able to decipher your intentions if you can't do it yourself.

Finally, journal entries can be morale boosters. Some of the most appropriate things you can record are answered prayers. Returning to these spiritual signposts during troubled times provides an opportunity for the gentle voice of the Holy Spirit to remind you, "See, I was there when this was happening, and I helped you through it. And look there—there's that time when you had a deadline to meet and I helped you write 100 pages in a week!"

Exercise

1. Purchase a notebook to use as a journal.

2. Tonight, write something about today. Describe an event that happened, a person you met, a place you went, a conversation you had, or just something you thought about, but write for at least five minutes.

3. Make it your goal to write in your journal for at least five minutes each day.

*H*old on to instruction, do not let it go.

Proverbs 4:13

*B*ooks on writing tend to make much of how difficult it is to become a successful writer, but the truth is that, though the ability to write well is partly a gift—like the ability to play basketball well, or to outguess the stock market—writing ability is mainly a product of good teaching supported by a deep-down love of writing.

John Gardner

*L*iterature is strewn with the wreckage of men who have minded beyond reason the opinion of others.

Virginia Woolf

Chapter: 4.

Help Along the Way

I was only eight years old, but already I was a failure. In most of those things that measure success for a third grader, I had failed.

I will never forget that afternoon. I was wearing my Brownie uniform. The rest of the girls from my class had gone joyfully to the Scout meeting, while I walked home alone, staring at my report card and trying very hard to figure out how I could break the news to my parents.

Math: C . . . not so bad. *Spelling: F* . . . disaster. *Reading: F* . . . major disaster. *Conduct: C* . . . oh, well. *Effort: E* . . . my life was over.

Earlier, a few of the kids had asked me what was wrong. Was I sick? My freckles must have stood out distinctly on my pale skin. I did feel sick. The teacher had called me lazy. One of the boys had called me stupid. Could I be both of those terrible things?

It was the blackest day of my eight-year-old life, for I knew I had disappointed my parents. Mama called me bright. Daddy called me his little "go-getter." Didn't this report card repudiate everything they believed about me?

That evening the three of us sat down together in the

front room. My sisters had done well on their report cards. Their marks had been an occasion of personal celebration for them at suppertime. And I had heard Daddy whisper to my oldest sister, "Don't say anything to Bodie. She feels bad enough. Mommy and I will handle it."

And they did handle it . . . with the kind of encouragement and understanding that I still remember thirty years later.

I could barely choke out the words "I'm sorry." A flood of tears erupted, and my mother took me in her arms in a warm hug.

"Daddy and I know you're not lazy. We are absolutely certain you are not stupid," Mama said firmly.

"Learning to read is harder for some people than it is for others," Daddy added. (Later I would learn that his own father had never been able to learn to read, in spite of the fact that he was an intelligent and capable man and the son of a doctor.)

In the 1950s they didn't know much about learning disabilities; often those who had them were simply labeled "lazy" or "slow." Something was wrong with the way I was perceiving the written language, but my parents were not quite sure what it was. Something needed to be done, and quickly, or I might never get beyond third grade.

My mother was angry at the teacher's comments about my *laziness,* and so she asked my father to handle the matter alone at the school. This was a terrible ordeal for me. Daddy stood quietly for a moment as the teacher recited my faults. *I was backward. I did not live up to my potential. I was more interested in entertaining the other students than I was in studying. . . .* Once again tears of shame streamed down my cheeks.

Daddy put his strong hand on my shoulder and replied, "You are wrong. Dead wrong. The only thing wrong with

Bodie's ability to learn is that she has the wrong teacher."
He pulled me close to him, and suddenly I felt *defended*
and *safe*!

The teacher expressed her disapproval and disagree-
ment again, but somehow her judgment did not cut me
as it had before. Afterward, Daddy took me outside the
classroom and knelt down with his hands on my arms.

"Your mommy and I don't believe any of what she
says, Bodie. We will find you somebody who really knows
how to teach. Don't worry. You will work hard, won't
you?"

I nodded, trying to ignore the fact that I had been
working hard and had gotten nowhere.

He patted me on the back with his gruff affection.
"Good. Then you'll be reading in no time!"

My father was teaching me an important lesson. The
lesson of persistence.

Don't give up. Okay, maybe you're working as hard
as you can and you're getting nowhere. If that's the case,
then take another look at the way you're working. What's
your approach? If one path to your goal is closed, then you
should turn and look for another path.

For me, that other path meant a different teacher. My
parents knew of a bright young woman who had just
finished her first year of teaching. Her name was Anita
Martin, and she reminded me of the actress Mary Martin
of *Peter Pan* fame! She was full of enthusiasm and praise
when I made even the smallest progress. Throughout the
summer she met with me every weekday morning.

"Phonics doesn't seem to help Bodie," she explained
to my mother. "Since phonics doesn't work, we'll simply
concentrate on word recognition!"

41

Flash cards. Memorization. Word recognition. Hour after hour we drilled. To this day phonics is difficult for me, and I am a dreadful speller (as my editors will attest). But that summer I learned to read. Then I learned to put my own thoughts on paper.

Someday in heaven I'm going to ask the Lord to play back the tape of all the people and circumstances that made me a writer.

In high school I was fortunate to have a gifted and sensitive literature teacher named June Gaede. During my freshman year I presented her with a poem for the class literature project. She smiled slightly as she read it, and I knew she knew what I had done.

"You can do better than this," she said gently. She knew I had copied the poem from another source, but she never came right out and called me the thief I was. Instead, she saw a little girl who was hungry to write and be published, and she helped me achieve that goal *honestly*.

When I was not assigned to Mrs. Gaede's classroom, when other teachers scrawled red ink across my papers, I always found myself heading for her desk at lunch hour. She was never too busy to talk or encourage me. Most of what I wrote during those early years was cornball and mediocre. But Mrs. Gaede (and my family) never held up my own mediocrity as a mirror for me! Instead, this wonderful teacher shared great works of literature with me, reading passages from the greatest authors of history, with gentle admonition and encouragement:

"See how he captured that moment?
Can you hear the way she used dialect here?
Now you give it a try!
That's it!
Yes! You can do it!"

Since my first disastrous years in grade school, I have

held the unshakable conviction that there is nothing worse than a bad teacher and nothing nearer to the heart of God than a good one!

God blessed me with parents who expected and demanded that I give my best to every effort. He gave me teachers who could see beyond my failings to my heart's desire: to be a writer. There was nothing I wanted more. But I could never have reached that goal alone.

Where to Find Help to Improve Your Writing Ability

I will be honest with you. It is tough to learn from a book. You may need more help and encouragement than I can give you through these brief pages. You may need to find a teacher (or teachers) who can lift your sights toward achievements you cannot imagine right now.

I took one creative writing class in college, and it was the pits. Nearly everything I submitted came back with endless, illegible, red scrawling.

When I finally deciphered these remarks, I realized that the instructor had an enormous ego problem. She was not trying to help me with *my* writing; she was trying to get me to write my story the way she would have written it. So I dropped the class.

In the final analysis, the only thing that will improve your writing ability is more writing. But it's also true that most of us need both the encouragement that comes from associating with others of similar interests and the instruction that comes from honest but gentle criticism.

Community or junior colleges usually offer writing courses. Sometimes these are creative writing classes taught by frustrated poets with overstimulated intellects and are of doubtful value. Often, however, you can find

43

some real writing-for-publication courses (I've taught them myself at our local college) that offer practical help on tailoring manuscripts for submission to publishers. If you are thinking of taking a particular course, try to get a recommendation or opinion from someone who has already taken it, or who has at least taken courses from that instructor. If this is not possible, see if you can audit a class session before you pay any fees.

Lest you think the entire purpose of this section is to warn you to watch out for unscrupulous instructors who will take your money and leave you with nothing but a lot of avant-garde musings, here's the other side of the issue: If you enroll in a writing course, expect it to hurt. Expect the effort of keeping up with the writing assignments to be demanding and the instructor to be uninterested in excuses, to the point of deafness. You should also expect it to be emotionally taxing, as papers over which you have perspired are returned to you with bloodstains! Steel yourself to listen to others when they offer their opinions about your work, and try to practice Christian charity when given a similar opportunity!

With that in mind, heed this small warning: *In the heart of many an insecure and incompetent student writer lurks the need to rip another writer's work to shreds in the name of critique!* This sort of ignorance has become a pet peeve of mine over the years as I have seen the damage that can be done to the struggling new writer. So beware and be wary.

I highly recommend classes that require you to research, write, and get into print! Is there a journalism class nearby? Take it, by all means!

Does your local high school produce a yearbook? Volunteer to help the advisor. You may go into the experience as blank as a wall, but I guarantee that when you finish you will understand *plenty* about publishing. Not only that, but the poor, overworked yearbook advisor will rise up and call you blessed for helping out! In addition, you will have a fuller appreciation for editors and deadlines after such an experience.

Writers' Groups and Conferences

Writing associations, conferences, and workshops can be valuable or a waste of time, depending on their makeup and requirements and your willingness to work and make demands on yourself. Some groups require completed or published works as part of the price of admission and offer active and helpful critique times. Others are only pleasant social gatherings of writers wanting to talk about what they "intend to do" or reciting the painful progress of their great novel, five years in the making!

Groups of writers who are serious about improving their craft will often host writing seminars with guest speakers. These meetings and their bigger cousins, writers' conferences, also vary widely in value, but generally have two advantageous features: short-term time commitment and a modest expense (usually). Just remember: A seminar is not intended to revolutionize your life. But if you pick up even one new idea that is immediately usable, it will have made an important contribution to your growth as a writer.

Christian writers' conferences are held in many areas around the country every year. Biola in Los Angeles, Moody Bible Institute in Chicago, and Mt. Hermon in northern California are but a few locations. The *Inspirational Writers' Market Guide* lists Christian writers conferences as well as a state-by-state list of writers groups. Make it your goal to attend one of these conferences, even if you are unable to pursue any other additional instruction.

A good writer's conference will benefit you in several ways:

- The spiritual impact on your life will be terrific.
- The basic skills you learn will be invaluable.
- And you won't come out of the sessions damaged in any way!

It is this last point I want to emphasize again. If you intend to seriously pursue writing, be *very* careful whom you trust with that desire. A good instructor will not knock the stuffing out of you when helping you work through your flaws. But if that does happen to you, pick up your stuffing and leave quickly!

*H*e who scorns instruction will pay for it, but he who respects a command is rewarded.

Proverbs 13;13

*N*either is a dictionary a bad book to read . . . it is full of sugestion—the raw material of possible poems and histories.

Ralph Waldo Emerson

*T*he secret of all good writing is sound judgment.

Horace

Chapter:

5.

The Writer's Market

*E*ach year Brock and I travel six hours to the annual San Francisco Library Book Sale. Held in an enormous warehouse in the Marina District, the sale provides some of the best bargains of the century.

We prowl from crate to crate, examining the books that have been donated to the library from estates or private collections during the previous twelve months. We have come away with first-edition Steinbecks and Mark Twains. With precious volumes of old Western lore published a hundred years ago.

On the way back home our car sits down on its haunches and groans at us. Our library bookshelves are packed and stacked tight.

All these books have provided important research material for our novels and our historical pieces for various magazines, but a handful are essential to my writing.

Any competent professional, whether doctor, engineer, or financial planner, collects a set of treasured reference volumes, and the professional writer is no different. Some of these, because of their direct connection to literature, will come as no surprise to you. Others on our short list may strike you as unexpected.

Collecting a Set of Reference Books

The first reference work you should acquire is a good dictionary. Dictionaries do much more than just provide correct spellings. They indicate shades of meaning, giving the writer the opportunity to check a particular usage for correctness of application. They provide correct variations on the initial word, such as plurals or negatives. Dictionaries are also handy for checking the meanings of unfamiliar words that turn up in research reading and interviews.

A second important reference book for writers is a thesaurus. A thesaurus is not a luxury. When writing about any subject, a specific set of words may easily become overworked to the point of irritation to the reader. A good thesaurus will supply a wealth of synonyms and will even aid you in distinguishing between similar but subtly different usages so that you can choose the one that best expresses your thoughts.

Next on the writer's bookshelf is an almanac. These annual fountains of information provide data on sporting events, grain harvests, Nobel prizes, and hit songs. As a source of current background information about all forms of human endeavor and popular culture, they are unequaled. Almanacs allow the writer to substantiate statements that might otherwise go unsupported, like "all Americans are influenced by television" (98% of U.S. homes own at least one set). Or how about this: "The Midwest is accurately called the Bible Belt" (five evangelical denominations are headquartered in Illinois and five more in Indiana, and eight in Missouri).

Another fundamentally important resource aid is a good set of encyclopedias. While these reference books are very general in nature, they supply accurate background information about historical figures and events. Moreover, they often point the researcher to related topics or lines of inquiry that might otherwise be overlooked. (Or did you think you got away from library drill when you left school?)

Of no less importance is the basic-basic reference book, *Writer's Market*. This annual is accurately subtitled "Where and How to Sell What You Write." We'll discuss this in detail in the next section, but just note here that you really can't proceed further as a professional free-lance writer without this volume, or its Christian counterpart, the *Inspirational Writers' Market Guide*.

Finally, there's your sword. Your Bible. Whether or not the publication for which you are writing will accept direct scriptural quotations is beside the point. If you truly believe that your heavenly Father is genuinely interested in all aspects of your life, whether family, money, recreation, or conscience, doesn't it make sense to consult His Word for the principles it has to offer about any subject on which you might write? You bet it does. In fact, the Bible itself says: "All Scripture is God-breathed and is useful for teaching, rebuking, correcting and training in righteousness, so that the man of God may be thoroughly equipped for every good work" (2 Tim. 3:16).

The Writer's Market

Each year I am first in line at my local bookstore to buy the newest edition of *Writer's Market*. I have copies on my shelf that date back twenty years, and all of them are dog-eared and scribbled on.

YOU CANNOT BE A PUBLISHED WRITER UNLESS YOU HAVE A CURRENT COPY OF *WRITER'S MARKET!*

I write these words on the blackboard of every classroom I enter as teacher or lecturer. My publisher will not appreciate my telling you this, but *Writer's Market* is more essential to your success than any book on writing you can buy.

If you do not own a copy of *Writer's Market,* you may as well stop reading now because the rest of this chapter, and much of the book, will not make sense without it.

Practice in Analyzing Periodicals

If you need a plumber, you have to know how to use the Yellow Pages. If you want to write or call someone, you have to know how to look up their address or phone number. And if you want to write for a magazine, you have to thoroughly understand its format, preferences, and habits. To get this information, you must know how to use *Writer's Market.*

To give you some practice in locating periodicals you are interested in writing for, we've selected a sampling of different publications, from general interest to very specific, from well-established to brand-new, both Christian and secular.

Let's begin with one of the best known of all magazines in the world, *National Geographic,* the publication of the National Geographic Society. Founded in 1890, this familiar yellow-bordered magazine has a circulation of more than 10,000,000!

The *Writer's Market* entry reads, in part, as follows: "Approximately 50% free-lance written. Prefers to work with published/established writers, and works with a small number of new/unpublished writers each year. . . . *National Geographic* publishes first-person, general interest, heavily illustrated articles on science, natural history, exploration and geographical regions. . . . Fewer than one percent of unsolicited queries result in assignments. Query (500 words) by letter, not by phone, to Senior Assistant Editor (Contract Writers). Do not send manuscripts. Before querying, study recent issues and check a *Geographic Index* at a library. . . . Seldom returns to regions or subjects covered within the past ten years."

Whew! Sounds tough, right? No argument there. But notice what a wealth of information we got about how to proceed and who will be successful. Now let's take a quick look at a recent issue of the magazine itself.

In it, we find six articles. One is a modern-day examination of the ancient route used by the Crusaders. One is a history of the religious sect called Shakers and an update on the few adherents who remain. A third discusses the contents of a recently opened box that was sealed shut one hundred years ago. Two articles concern geographical regions: the nation of Malawi and a special report on conservation efforts in the Himalayas. The final piece is in the natural history realm and deals with an unusual form of aphids.

In this particular issue none of the articles are by first-time writers. Two of the pieces are by Geographic staff members, and the other four writers are noted as having written for the magazine before. Interestingly, the photographic credits indicate that some of the contributors in this issue are new to the *Geographic*. Excluding the two articles written by magazine staffers, the pieces range in length from 2500 words to 6500 and are accompanied by 15 to 30 illustrations each.

Let's now turn to a sports-related periodical, *Skin Diver* magazine. *Writer's Market* reports that this publication is 85% free-lance written and that they are "eager to work with new/unpublished writers." Isn't that encouraging? The entry also indicates that they accept articles in the areas of "foreign and domestic travel, recreation, ocean exploration, scientific research, commercial diving and technological development." More practical and specific advice is contained in the phrase, "Buys 200 mss/year. Send complete ms. Length: 300–2000 words; 1200 preferred."

A brief review of an issue of the magazine shows 30 different articles, not including the columns and features written by magazine staffers. Now, lest you get too excited about this golden opportunity, about half of the articles were written by staff members or "contributing editors" (authors who write for the magazine on a regular basis). Still, this means that about 15 were written by free-lancers, including 2 written by one author, and 3 by another.

Several of the stories are in first-person form, and the travel articles follow a very identifiable pattern. First they give an overview of the location, then examine the various dive sites to be found there, along with their attractions, and finally conclude with information about travel arrangements and accommodations.

———

Next we'll look at a Christian publication, *Christian Parenting Today*. This magazine is too new to have an entry in *Writer's Market*, so our analysis will be confined to what we can learn from examining the magazine itself.

The masthead mentions that "unsolicited manuscripts are accepted; however a query letter is preferred. . . . Enclose SASE, please." Eight names are listed as columnists, and 23 more are called contributing editors. This particular issue contains 14 feature articles.

A quick study shows that the free-lance pieces run from 1000 to 2000 words, with 1500 being the norm. What this means to you as a prospective contributor is that your manuscript will be more likely to get favorable reception if it adequately treats the subject in about 1500 words, and would be less likely to be acceptable if it were, say, 4000 words.

A careful analysis of the articles in this issue shows the following broad groupings: "Teaching kids about . . ."; first-person inspirational pieces ("I learned God's love through . . ."); and "Selecting . . . for children."

Another possibility that suggests itself is a short-short piece, 500 words or less, with directions for a special recipe or a craft project to make with kids.

Are you beginning to see how you can sense a magazine's "personality" from the information in *Writer's Market* and from spending some time reviewing a sample copy of the publication itself? Think of yourself as a salesperson with a great many products (story ideas) to sell. Having a quality item is not enough. You must make sure, to the best of your ability, that your manuscript fills a need *and* is presented in a form that will make the buyer (publisher or editor) say, "I can see this fitting our publication."

Shall we take a look at another example? How about a national, general-interest publication, *Travel and Leisure*. I've purposely selected this one to offset some of the discouragement you may have felt after checking out the *National Geographic*. With a circulation of over 1,000,000, you might think that this publication would be very finicky and, therefore, be tempted to pass right by without seriously regarding it as a possibility. But look what the *Writ-*

er's Market reports: "80% free-lance written. . . . Buys 200 mss/year." Its entry also supplies this tip: "Read the magazine. Regionals and Taking Off sections are best places to start."

Sound advice is golden! The regional section contains three articles of about 1000 words each. They are travel pieces that pertain to specific parts of the country (near you, maybe?) and can be very focused in their scope. How about this: The attractions and accommodations available at *one* little-known lake! The key to making such an article acceptable? *Has it been done before, and if so, how recently?*

The other suggested section, Taking Off, appears even less intimidating. The sample issue contains twelve short (200 to 1000 words) offerings, each reporting on one city or even one restaurant or hotel!

Finally, let's look at one more avowedly Christian publication, *Moody Monthly.* Our trusty, and by now familiar, *Writer's Market* lets us in on the information that the magazine is 20% free-lance written, with an expected purchase of 50 manuscripts per year. We are told that these are "how-to's on living the Christian life, humor and personal experience." Listen to how specific the advice is in regard to first-person articles: "The only article [in the magazine] written for non-Christians; a personal testimony written by the author (we will accept 'as told to's'); the objective is to tell a person's testimony in such a way that the reader will understand the gospel and want to accept Christ as Savior." In this area the magazine buys 30 manuscripts each year and these should be between 750 and 1200 words long.

The sample issue reviewed contains 12 articles. One is a personal testimony, two are testimonies of Christian "personalities," another is a Bible study with practical applications. Most were in the specified 1200-word range.

Exercises

Now it's your turn. With a magazine in hand and the *Writer's Market* open to the appropriate page, begin your own analysis.

1. Compare the authors' names to the masthead list of magazine staffers and contributing editors. Does the proportion of free-lance material fit the percentage given in *Writer's Market?*

2. How many articles are there? Check the length of several. Do they average out to the suggested word count?

3. What type of pieces are included? How-to, interviews, descriptive, narrative, or what?

4. Are any written first person? If so, which ones, and how would you characterize them?

5. Does a certain type of selection seem to require a specific length?

We'll be looking at specifics of style, sentence structure, and vocabulary a little later, but for now, can you get a feel for the publication? Is it folksy or aloof? Simple and straightforward or complex and intellectual?

Now the $64,000 question: Can you locate at least one article about which you can say, "I could have written that," or better still, "I could have done a better job writing that, because I would have . . ."? If so, congratulations! Seeing yourself as a contributor is an important step toward actually being one. If you can't, try to determine why you feel that way. In any case, select one magazine with which you feel most comfortable, not just in regard to subject matter, but in terms of what the *Writer's Market* indicates and your own sense of what is required.

*T*herefore, since we are surrounded by such a great cloud of witnesses. . . .

Hebrews 12:1

*I*nformation's pretty thin stuff, unless mixed with experience.

Clarence Day

*T*here is no subject so old that something new cannot be said about it.

Fyodor Dostoyevski

Chapter:

6.

What Are Your Interests?

*H*e is my first memory. A sun-weathered, lean giant almost 6'4" tall. My great-grandfather. He called me "Little Billie," after a daughter he had lost thirty years before, and he reached down and hefted me up and up and up onto his shoulder. I wrapped my fingers in his thick gray hair and held on tightly as he sauntered out toward the corral, where the rest of the family stood admiring the big golden horse inside the round pen.

Nearly forty years later, my mother is amazed that I remember that day with such accuracy. I was not much more than two years old. I could hardly talk. But I remember everything . . .

Clipper's soft velvet nose poked through the rails of the fence. Great-Grandpa guided my hand to touch it. The horse nickered gently. Great-Grandpa set me on the top rail of the fence beside my daddy, and then the old man and Clipper performed for us. On cue, the horse nodded and bowed. He pawed out his age in the ground. He pulled a red kerchief from Great-Grandpa's pocket and waved it like a flag.

Then, in a moment of magic, my great-grandfather again reached out for me and I sailed through the air and landed on the broad, warm back of the horse. I was not afraid. I never wanted to get off. Around and around we circled the corral, and when at last they took me down, I cried to be put back on Clipper again.

As I look back on it now, it seems as though that first memory marks the beginning of my life, the awakening of all the things I enjoy most. From the earthy smells of the barnyard to the sloppy licks of the stock-dogs, it all stayed with me to direct my life as an adult, as a parent, and as a writer.

Before I ever learned to read, Mama read me nearly every horse book she could find. I marveled at the story of *Black Beauty* and listened spellbound to the tales of *The Black Stallion*. Writers like Louis L'Amour came into my life later. And the films of John Wayne and director John Ford were my favorites at the Saturday matinees.

I never imagined that one day I would share a cup of coffee with Louis L'Amour, or sit across a table from John Wayne and laugh with him about some story from the "good old days." They were great men. Truly great and wonderful men. Their memories were rooted in the sweet smell of hay and the warm hide of a horse. They carried a deep love of the lore of the West, and this was reflected in their work and in their lives.

It is amazing that such basic things directed my footsteps to the offices of John Wayne Enterprises, but as a young writer I wisely followed my interests. I wrote for equine magazines. When I was not sitting at a typewriter, I was sitting on the back of a horse. Even now when I need a change of pace I call up one of the editors of an equine publication and get an assignment for an article that interests me.

The West. That is where I began, and I find I have not wandered from my beginnings at all.

The point of this is quite simple: God has instilled in each of our hearts a unique and special set of memories and perspectives. Your interests may well be the path God has put you on in order for you to write about men and women you have only dreamed of meeting. Ask yourself what it is that you enjoy most. Whatever it is, no doubt there is a magazine that covers the topic. Why not write for it?

Whatever your hopes as a writer, follow your heart. Examine the unique set of memories and experiences that make you who you are. Then ask yourself which of those interests might be pursued and somehow used through the written word to serve the kingdom of God.

From my earliest childhood I loved horses. So I began writing for equine magazines. And, as they say, the rest is history . . .

Right now sit down and make a list of all the things you are interested in; include interests you consider secular or even unimportant. After all, God is concerned about every detail of your life. He might use something you consider trivial and insignificant to further His own work.

Then, with your list of interests completed, it is time to make a trip to the newsstand.

Topic Selection—Broad Planning

Stroll into your neighborhood pharmacy and spend a few minutes in front of the magazine rack. What do you notice first? Probably that a great number of different publications are striving to attract your attention. I recently completed this exercise myself and discovered that there were (care to guess?) *seventy* different titles represented. And this was by no means a large newsstand nor a particularly diverse selection.

The next day I reviewed the display at an airport news counter and found forty publications, many of them totally different from those at the drugstore. Another trip, this time to a bookstore with a well-stocked and comprehensive magazine section, produced a count of well over one hundred different periodicals!

The second observation that comes to mind when you check out the local magazine rack is the degree to which the publications reach into minute and specific areas. Take for instance the subject "parenting and home life." My pharmacy displayed eight different publications related to this area, not counting the ones shown near the checkout stand. I saw four different magazines on shooting, two on photography, four on computers (including one that dealt specifically with the use of a computer as part of an at-home office), and ten on auto customizing and racing!

In addition to general sports magazines, there are magazines on running, swimming, skiing, skin diving, and golf. Besides general health magazines, there are magazines on nutrition, exercise, aerobics, and how to extend your life expectancy! Are you beginning to get the drift? Not only is there enormous opportunity for getting published, but there are almost certainly several periodicals that will match up with hobbies and interests you already possess. Isn't that terrific?

The proper question for you to be asking as you contemplate the magazine rack is not *How can I get published?* but *Which of these desperate editors will be most anxious to hear from me?*

Exercise

Select at least three magazines on a topic in which you already have some interest and involvement, or at least some knowledge of the terminology. What's that you say? You can't think of any?

Do you participate in any sports? Do you cook or sew? Do you travel or camp? Do you live somewhere? Chances are there's a regional magazine for your part of the world.

Try to concentrate on one area of interest. But if you're uncertain, choose three different topics and review the appropriate magazines to see which subject appeals to you the most.

Example: I'm interested in horses, having owned several over the years. On the newsstand I find *Horseman Magazine* and *The Western Horseman.* Turning to my *Writer's Market* I discover that the former has a circulation of 140,000 and buys 100 articles a year. A note adds that about 60% are free-lance written. *The Western Horseman* suggests that they "work with a small number of new/unpublished writers each year" and that the circulation is 162,369.

Example: I seem to have a flair for landscaping and gardening projects. Is there a magazine market for this? You bet! How about *Better Homes and Gardens* (10–15% free-lance written), *Flower and Garden Magazine* (50% free-lance written, buys 20–30 manuscripts a year), or *National Gardening* (85% free-lance written, buys 80–100 manuscripts a year)?

Example: My next-door neighbor is a pro football player and a terrific Christian. Could I interview him for a magazine? How about *Moody Monthly* (20% free-lance written), *Christianity Today* (80% free-lance written), or *Guideposts* (30% free-lance written)?

Exercise

For each of the magazines you have selected, consult the *Writer's Market* listing and make notes. From each magazine's contents, develop an analysis of who the contributors are and the nature, style, and length of the freelance pieces.

*I*n the beginning was the Word. . . .

John 1:1

*I*f you went to work for a newspaper that required you to write two or three articles every day, you would be a better writer after six months. You wouldn't necessarily be writing well—your style might still be pedestrian, full of clutter and cliches. But at least you would be exercising your powers of putting the English language on paper, gaining confidence, and identifying the commonest problems.

*A*ll writing is ultimately a question of solving a problem. It may be a problem of where to obtain the facts, or how to organize the material. It may be a problem of approach or attitude, tone or style. Whatever it is, it has to be confronted and solved.

William Zinsser

Chapter:

7.

W, W, W, W, W, and H

So this was writer's block. Every part of my brain had turned to Jell-o. I sat staring at the keys of my old Smith-Corona as if they were going to tell me where to start. The blank piece of paper had been rolled onto the carriage so long that it was now permanently pressed into a curve.

Every other reporter had finished the morning's assignments long ago. The blue haze of cigarette smoke hung over the room like gun powder after a battle. It appeared that I was the only casualty in this daily war of words. *Where do I begin???*

At the sound of approaching footsteps, I looked up . . . it was the City Editor. Was it too late to dive under my desk? His scowling face cut through my paralyzed mind. My lips formed the words, "Hi, Eddie."

Still scowling, he flicked the edge of my blank paper. "Whatsa matter, kid? You got writer's block?"

I nodded. Actually it was more like the Berlin Wall. The Iron Curtain of all writer's blocks. "I can't figure out where to start," I said quietly.

"Who you trying to be? Hemingway? So just write it already."

"But—"

"Don't they teach you kids anything in school?" he growled, and stuck out his lip in disapproval of all journalism programs. "The best writer in the world isn't gonna get anywhere without basic stuff. The *basics!* That's the key that's gonna crack those words out of the vault! There's not a newsman in here that doesn't freeze up once in a while. *Basics!* That's what'll get you back to the story!" With that, Eddie stalked away, leaving me alone with a looming deadline and his terse advice.

Within seconds I had gone through my mental file card of journalism basics: *Five Ws and the H. Elements of lead paragraph. Begin the first line with either a (1) statement, (2) quote, (3) question, or (4) description.*

It took me just about that long to start typing. (I began my story with a statement.) I finished the first line before Eddie was out the door. I hesitated just long enough to glance up and shrug as the gruff old bulldog gave me his *atta-girl* nod. Then he was off to the coffee room and I was writing.

When he got back, my nine-column-inch story was on his desk. The hard lead paragraph contained the five Ws and the H. It was written in the classic inverted-pyramid style, and it was finished with six minutes to spare on the deadline.

Eddie edited it in a minute and a half, then sent it off to typesetting.

That newspaper is buried in some dusty archive now, but the lessons I learned from that experience in the newsroom are with me every time I sit down to write.

The question I am asked most frequently at writers' seminars is this: "How can you possibly produce 700 manuscript pages in four months?"

My answer is always the same. "I am a journalist."

Before you accuse me of being too cryptic, let me explain a little more. A news reporter often writes two or more stories a day. Let's say those pieces average 5 pages each, making a total of 10 pages for each working day. If a reporter works twenty days a month, that means he or she has produced 200 pages of written material in that month. Multiply that number by four months and you end up with 800 pages. Which means that the ordinary news journalist surpasses my production.

All of this is just to let you know that there are no mystical secrets to get you past the *wanting-to-write* point. Everything you need to know in order to write successfully can be found in the *basics of journalism*. And these are skills I have taught, successfully, to my son's seventh-grade class.

So you wanna be a writer? Well, this is where you start. With the basics.

———

I first heard about the *5 Ws and the H* in Mr. Schuler's seventh-grade journalism class.

"If you want to be a writer, you have to learn to ask six questions!" The crusty old teacher wrote them on the board for us.

WHO?

WHAT?

WHEN?

WHERE?

WHY?

HOW?

All writing centers around asking these questions and

then answering them for your reader. All *really* good writing is just that basic and that simple to understand.

Pick up a magazine. Scan through the articles. You will see these six questions answered within each article.

Some stories may put more emphasis on the WHO. Others may deal heavily with the WHAT or the WHY or the HOW of a particular story. But the six questions I memorized in seventh grade are the foundation of all writing.

These six questions will also be the foundation of every interview you have and every piece you produce for publication. If you write a novel, you will find that these six little questions are vital to your plot line. If you develop a weekly newsletter for your church or school, you will be amazed at how much material will be hung from the framework of the *5 Ws and the H.*

With that in mind, I'm going to let you in on a secret: The Lord is a journalist! He is the original teacher who stressed the importance of answering these six questions for readers.

You don't believe me? I'm pushing the point a bit far, you say? Just for fun, let's take a look at the structure of the first few verses of the gospel of John. Open your Bible and answer each question with a word or a phrase from the listed verse.

John 1:1

1. When? ....
....
....

2. Who? ....
....
....

3. Where? ....

70

John 1:4
4. What? ....

....

....

John 1:7
5. Why? ....

....

....

John 1:12
6. How? ....

....

....

Again and again throughout the Scriptures we see these six basic questions being answered with a ringing clarity that reaches deep into the questioning heart of humanity. These questions and answers, phrased in hundreds of different ways, have touched millions of souls over thousands of years through the written Word.

> *WHEN?*   *In the beginning . . .*
>
> *WHO?*   *The Word . . .*
>
> *WHERE?*   *Was with God . . .*
>
> *WHAT?*   *In him was life; and that life was the light of men . . .*
>
> *WHY?*   *That through him all men might believe . . .*
>
> *HOW?*   *To all who received him, to those who believed in his name, he gave the right to become children of God.*

For a lost and questioning world, Jesus Christ is the answer to the six questions in the heart of every person. Basic journalism, plain and simple.

For those of us entrusted with the honor of sharing God's love through the written word, it is important that we remember the Lord's first law of journalism: *Great Truth is taught in simple ways.* And if *the Word* himself uses the *5 Ws and the H* as the framework for His book, maybe we need to pay attention.

You may write for a travel magazine or an off-road vehicle publication or a tabloid. Your topic could be the story of someone's survival in a hurricane or the heroic struggle of a child with a terminal illness. Whatever you write, make these six questions the foundation of your work, and you will produce a well-crafted story, worthy of publication.

A truthful witness does not deceive.

Proverbs 14:5

*W*ords—so innocent and powerless as
they are, as standing in a dictionary, how potent
for good and evil they become in the hands of one
who knows how to combine them.

Nathaniel Hawthorne

*L*iterature is the art of writing something that will be read twice; journalism, what will
be grasped at once.

Cyril Connolly

Turkey Carcass Writing

*M*uch has been made of the fact that I was writing for a newspaper by the time I was sixteen. Too much, I think. I was the lowliest of the low. I was "the *kid*." Maybe I thought I was big-time stuff then, but the truth is that I was paid by the column inch. Fifty cents for every column inch that made it into print.

I laugh about it now, but I remember trying not to watch as my copy passed into the hands of the editor and he began "to edit." Actually, it was a lot like watching my father carve up a turkey. Off came wings, drumsticks, great slices of white meat, until finally all that remained was the carcass. Bare bones. Usually it was the skeleton of my effort that ended up crammed into the available space.

"What's wrong, kid?" Berg would ask.

"Ah, nothing. I just watched my paycheck shrink from twelve bucks to six, that's all."

"That was pretty good stuff you wrote about the rivalry between North and South High schools being like the Battle of Bull Run. Too bad it ended up in the can. Just not enough space today."

Inverted Pyramid
"Just the facts, Ma'am!"

"Yeah. I know. *Inverted pyramid,* right?"

"*Inverted pyramid.* You got it. It's a killer for you stringers."

The inverted pyramid style of writing was indeed murder to my meager paycheck, but it was, and still is, the only way all those stories could be easily trimmed to fit into the limited space of the newspaper.

Briefly, this technique requires the writer to put the broadest and most general information in the very first paragraph, called the "hard lead" paragraph. These brief but comprehensive lines must contain most of the *5 Ws and the H.*

The paragraphs that follow the hard lead contain details that flesh out the story, such as quotes from eyewitnesses, descriptions of a gun battle, or details of a high-level conference of heads of state. All of this information may be important, but if the newspaper needs to make room for more advertising or additional stories, then those paragraphs must be cut to make that space.

Starting from the bottom (the end of the story), the editor begins to cut away at the paragraphs following the lead. Sometimes all that remains is that one little lead paragraph containing the essential facts.

Take a look at the front page of your hometown newspaper. Nearly every story will be structured in this inverted, or upside down, pyramid style.

When diagrammed, news stories should look like the Inverted Pyramid diagram. The editor may easily cut these stories from the bottom paragraph up.

Learning Your Craft—Basic Elements

Your daily newspaper is the very best textbook for this style of writing.

A newspaper's stock-in-trade is its ability to grab readers' attention, then satisfy their initial curiosity with the Jack Webb treatment ("Just the facts, ma'am") while hinting that those who are interested in pursuing a given subject will find it well worth their time to read on.

This is journalism in its purest form. I called it "Turkey Carcass Writing" because usually all that remained of my wonderful, strutting, preening, full-feathered story was a pile of bones!

77

As painful as this style of writing can be at times, it is essential that you understand and master it. It is the mark of an excellent craftsman when the first few lines of a hard lead news story are both informative and interesting!

Exercise

Get a newspaper. A large circulation, world-acclaimed daily or a modest, hometown offering, it makes no difference.

1. Starting with page one, analyze the opening paragraphs of each story.

2. Circle the hard lead paragraphs that contain most of the 5 Ws and the H.

3. Beside each paragraph you have circled, list the questions that have been answered: Who, What, When, Where, Why, and How.

4. Choose one news story that is written in the inverted pyramid style. Beginning with the last paragraph, cut the story in half. Then read to see if any really important details have been eliminated.

5. Write a hard lead paragraph containing the *5 Ws and the H* announcing the birth of your mother.

*A*lways be prepared to give an answer to everyone who asks you to give the reason for the hope that you have. But do this with gentleness and respect. . . .

1 Peter 3:15

I always do the first line well, but I have trouble doing the others.

Moliére

*T*he most important sentence in any article is the first one. If it doesn't induce the reader to proceed to the second sentence, your article is dead. And if the second sentence doesn't induce him to continue to the third sentence, it's equally dead. Of such a progression of sentences, each tugging the reader forward until he is safely hooked, a writer constructs that fateful unit: the "lead."

William Zinsser

Pick One and Write!

Over the years I did more Turkey Carcass Writing than I can even remember. Sorting through collections of old magazine articles, I found one example called "Alfalfa, Drought, and Your Feed Bill." Basic journalism. Hard lead. Inverted pyramid style. A real work of art. No doubt some interested rancher spotted the catchy title and devoured every scrap of information!

What I remember most about that story is the paycheck. I was pregnant with our first baby when I plucked that envelope out of the mailbox and waddled happily back to show my husband. We went out to dinner, and I felt very contented that I had written something and been paid for it!

Times were lean. Brock was student teaching and working part time. We had a nine-year-old car that always needed repairs. So a check for seventy-five dollars was a very big deal.

And I owed it all to the *5 Ws and the H!* Hard lead. Inverted pyramid. That bit of knowledge helped take the edge off our first struggling years as newlyweds. I wrote and wrote and sold and sold. Nothing fancy nor dramatic.

Just basic news-story articles. Meat and potatoes and . . . lots of turkey carcasses!

During this time I was writing other things as well. On a TV tray I scribbled out my first play in longhand.

It was a comedy, and all I cared about was that the audience laughed at the right places. Sitting in the back of the theater and watching my words come to life was one of the high points of my first twenty years on earth!

Teachers who had scribbled "trite" on my essays now came around to tell me I had been their most promising pupil. They were lying. I was a terrible student and had made their lives miserable, but all that was forgiven when *the play* was produced.

I submitted it in a contest. It won. A check came in the mail. Brock and I were thrilled. The money paid a car repair bill with enough left over for Kentucky Fried Chicken and a drive-in movie.

I wrote another play.

Writing is, for the most part, a solitary profession, offering hardly a nod of recognition. Nineteen years later I still believe that no professional experience quite rivals the fun of listening to a live audience applaud your work. Those hours of watching rehearsals and then sensing the enjoyment of the audience were the pat on the head God must have known I needed. His nod of encouragement, leading me on to other things . . .

———

I broadened my market and published with a number of different magazines. Basic journalism stuff. Interviews. Human interest pieces. How-to articles and straight news. These not only helped pay the bills but allowed us some extras.

Branching out with a number of publications also

meant the opportunity to move from Turkey Carcass Writing to a less rigid structure, from the hard lead opening to what is known as the soft lead.

I suppose it is called "soft" because it does not whack the reader over the head with a sack of hard facts. While the soft lead must still be a powerful attention-getter, it leads the reader more gently into the story.

The soft lead is most commonly used in magazine writing and may begin in one of four ways:

1. *Question:* "Where were you when the great earthquake struck San Francisco?"

2. *Quote:* "I couldn't believe it was happening," Alicia Thomas whispered quietly. "We were on the freeway driving back to Oakland when suddenly the road began to rock! I looked in my rearview mirror and the entire upper deck was collapsing."

3. *Description:* "The ground beneath Candlestick Park began to tremble as the crowd sat in shocked, fearful silence. Cracks formed in the concrete bleachers, and men and women ducked beneath the seats as chunks of concrete rained down."

4. *Statement:* "No one who was in San Francisco that day will forget the awesome power of the Great Quake of 1989."

Question . . . Quote . . . Description . . . Statement.

Take a moment to memorize those four little words and you will never experience the horrible panic that screams, *"Where do I begin?"*

Pick one. Any one of the four will do. Toss a coin if you have to. The point is, you will never again need to sweat over the beginning of a magazine article (or a short story or a novel). You simply choose one and . . . *begin!*

Writing a feature or human interest story for a magazine still requires that you answer most of those six questions found in the *5 Ws and the H*. However, the entire structure of the piece will be different from a news story.

The feature begins with a soft lead. From this interest-catching opener it builds, telling the story with quotes or facts or description. The conclusion of the feature story climaxes with the most important or interesting information. When diagramed, the feature story looks like this:

Upright Pyramid
The Feature Story

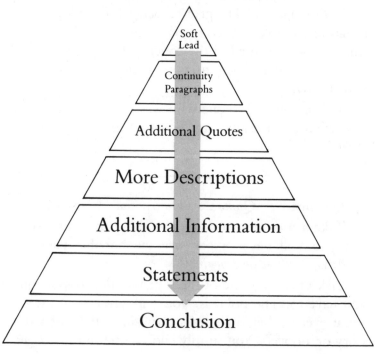

By the conclusion of the article, the central paragraphs answer the *5 Ws and the H* through the use of quotes, descriptions, and statement (see diagram).

Learning Your Craft

Your best textbook for the feature is the magazine you want to write for. Take a few moments to scan the articles in a current issue. There may be a few hard lead stories, but for the most part you will find features that include human interest stories and how-to articles.

Pick one feature that interests you. Read the article paragraph by paragraph, making notes in the side margin, answering the following:

1. Is it hard or soft lead?

2. If the opening paragraph is a soft lead, which technique did the writer use? Question, Quote, Description, or Statement?

3. Identify a paragraph containing each of the following: Quote, Statement, Description, Facts.

4. In each paragraph, identify which elements of the *5 Ws and the H* are present.

5. As a reader, why did you enjoy the article?

6. What makes the conclusion powerful?

7. Rewrite the lead paragraph with material from the main body of the article. Use one of the four methods: Question, Quote, Description, or Statement.

*W*hoever loves discipline loves knowledge.

Proverbs 12:1

*J*ust as our eyes need light in order to see, our minds need ideas in order to conceive.

Nicolas Malebranche

*I*f the idea is good, it will survive defeat, it may even survive victory.

Stephen Vincent Benét

Chapter:

10.

Clip Clippings, Not Coupons

Beneath our bed lodge several cardboard boxes. Within those boxes are old manuscripts—books and scripts and magazine articles—thousands of pages. Brock says that the only way writers can rest on their laurels is if the laurels are under the bed. So . . . that's where we keep our manuscripts.

The truth is, that once you are a writer, there will hardly be a moment in your working life when you can rest on past accomplishments. I learned that early on.

I was a young writer, working for John Wayne Enterprises, doing what the boss called "O.J.T."—*On-the-Job Training*. One of my first assignments was to research and interview old writers and directors who had made their mark on the movie industry in the "golden days" of Hollywood. How I loved that task! Brock often went with me, and we marveled at the opportunity we had been given. To actually get to know the scriptwriters who had written great movies for men like Clark Gable and Gary Cooper and John Wayne! To hear about their experiences firsthand! To sit hour after hour with such luminaries as Henry Hathaway, who directed *True Grit,* and John Lee

Mahan, who wrote the script for Steinbeck's *Tortilla Flat!*

But as we entered the homes and apartments of these creative and magnificent people, I often felt a sense of sadness. Tarnished Oscars sat on dusty shelves. A tribute to faded glory. The industry had passed these men and women by, and even while still living they were forgotten.

The people I interviewed were in their seventies and eighties then. Most are gone now, but I hold their stories close to my heart, even though I cannot say or write much about that time in my career. The information I gleaned from those living remnants of history does not belong to me, and the contracts I signed stipulated that I could not share it publicly.

What I can share with you is the valuable lesson they taught me, and that is that a writer cannot ever rest on past accomplishments. The minute you quit working, you become history and are soon forgotten.

The films those artists produced are still great films. Many have never been surpassed in quality. But even so, they are history now.

One writer we met was nearly eighty when we last spoke with him. "I have at least fifty ideas up on my corkboard," he smiled. "I'll have to live to be 150 years old to write them all!"

That man was Louis L'Amour.

Louis was already in his forties when John Wayne bought the movie rights to one of his magazine stories, "Gift of Cochise." This was the basis for the film *Hondo*. Louis then expanded the story into a full-length Western, and his first American novel was born. (We were privileged to hear both Duke and Louis tell the story of that first great success! And what a story it is!)

The point is that men like Louis L'Amour and John Wayne continued to work and create until the end of their lives. Both achieved their greatest successes in their later years, while many of their colleagues were wasting away in dusty rooms filled with memories. Both received special congressional gold medals recognizing their ongoing achievements. Duke had a script in the works when he passed away, and Louis L'Amour was working on galley proofs the night before he died!

I remember those men with love and gratitude! They taught me that every day is a new beginning, every task an opportunity to use my creativity. And when I die I want to have a set of new galley proofs at my bedside and at least fifty new ideas on my corkboard!

Building a Clippings File

Where do ideas come from? Certainly they emerge from our God-given creativity and imagination, and as believers we quite properly give thanks to the Lord for His inspiration. But what is the source for the raw material of ideas? Where does the basic idea come from on which the inspiration can act?

Free-lance writers discover early on the practical and enduring value of a newspaper and magazine clippings file. Remember the sample advice we reviewed from *Writer's Market* about selecting and writing on a local topic with universal appeal? Well, I selected that example because it is one of the most common tips that editors and publishers give to prospective authors. Over and over again they suggest, "Don't set your sights on trying to report some earth-shaking news; you probably can't get there first anyway. Don't attempt to lecture on universal truth; you don't have the credentials. Instead, look for real people who are finding real solutions to real problems and tell their stories in as entertaining a way as possible." This is the clearest direction for the use, maintenance, and perfection of a clippings file.

Take a look at some examples from the local section of just one edition of a daily paper.

Example: The local police force expects to call up reserve officers for special duty on Halloween because last year the holiday produced arson, vandalism, and looting. A local police official and an officer of the Chamber of Commerce both commented that the trend toward violence on Halloween has been growing for several years. Do you think other communities have had similar experiences? Might the individuals quoted in the newspaper be available for further interviews on the subject? Can you see how an article about a local happening could be turned into one of national interest?

Example: The state's Education Board listened to the opposing views of Christian fundamentalists and civil libertarians about a revision of the state's guidelines that offers a stronger pro-evolution statement than ever before. The article noted that the state standards don't have the force of law but have historically been accepted as mandates by local school boards (story idea?) and that state guidelines influence textbook publishers (another story idea?). Furthermore, the article contained a quote from Rev. Louis Sheldon of the Traditional Values Coalition. Might he be available for an interview?

Example: The same section contained a brief article about the formation of a task force to investigate an apparent cancer cluster among the children of a tiny community nearby. Article ideas: early detection of childhood cancers; possible link between pesticides and cancer; drinking water contamination and the safety of your community's water supply.

All these articles appeared in one section from one paper on one day!

Now you may be thinking, "But I'm not interested in writing about Halloween, evolution, or childhood cancer." That's okay. The point is, all of these news items contained stories involving local people with real-life struggles. Undoubtedly someone will be inspired to pursue one of these reports and develop it into a publishable piece that thousands of readers in other parts of the country will be able to relate to, sympathize with, and be concerned about.

Think of each clipping as a springboard: A report captures your attention, suggesting a couple different approaches to a story that interests you. This points you to further reading or even directly to interviews. Depending on the subject, the context, and the magazine to which you are submitting the piece, *one* interview might be enough to furnish information for an entire article.

As certain reports catch your attention, cut them out of the paper, carefully noting the name of the paper and the date the story appeared. Place the clippings in folders labeled with the topics: Evolution, Abortion, Halloween. As you discover additional articles about each topic, cut them out and add them to the folders. Review the contents periodically to see what story ideas suggest themselves and what further sources of information are available.

In addition to providing you with story ideas, a clippings file will help you learn to analyze trends. Watch the progression of events from month to month, year to year. Do you see patterns emerging? Is Halloween vandalism becoming more violent? Suppose someone had kept a clippings file on abortion for the last ten years. Wouldn't that person be well-prepared to begin writing articles, or even a book, on the topic?

Exercises

1. List five possible sources from which you can draw for your clippings file.

1. ....
....
....
2. ....
....
....
3. ....
....
....
4. ....
....
....
5. ....
....
....

2. Clip at least three articles on topics of interest from today's newspaper. Place them in folders labeled according to subject. Make notes about possible story ideas that occur to you.

3. Spend an hour each week updating and adding to your clippings file. Review for story ideas, especially if you see a trend developing.

If any of you lacks wisdom, he should ask God, who gives generously to all without finding fault, and it will be given to him.

James 1:5

*Y*ou don't write because you want to say something; you write because you've got something to say.

F. Scott Fitzgerald

Making a Perfect Match

*T*he whole thing started as a challenge.

"Get published in *American West* magazine? Ha! You've got to be a Pulitzer prize winner! You've got to be Louis L'Amour or Steinbeck or . . . somebody." She hurled these words at me over coffee one morning at the local cafe.

I countered the dare. "I have more chance of getting published in *American West* than Steinbeck does!"

"Oh yeah?"

"Yeah. Steinbeck's dead and I'm not."

I had her there. Maybe I hadn't won a Pulitzer, but at least I was breathing.

"There's not a magazine in the whole country that's harder to get into than *American West.*"

She was right. Hard was not the word. A bimonthly magazine sponsored by the Buffalo Bill Cody Museum, *American West* is sort of a scaled-down *Smithsonian*. Each year they publish maybe forty articles out of thousands of submissions. Yes. Trying to break into this magazine was something like trying to break into the vault of Chase-

Manhattan Bank: You had to know the combination of several locks.

"I can do it," I said. "What have Pulitzer prize winners got that I haven't got? Besides fame and money and respect?"

My friend smiled sarcastically. "Well, you've got more hot air than all of 'em put together . . . *American West,* my eye!"

I cannot count the times I regretted taking up the gauntlet of her scorn. She did not believe that a writer of my youth and inexperience could get past the slush pile. And I wasn't about to admit that I was not really all that sure myself.

My first task was to study the magazine. I did that, dismayed to see that she was right about the list of Pulitzer prize winners and notable authors. Every author was a *somebody*! Each either had scores of books to his or her credit or was head of this university department or that historical society. I was intimidated, but determined.

My second task was to choose a topic. So what did I know about the American West? Well, first of all, I lived there, and I had gathered some great stories from the old cowboys. I also had a good friend who was a Navajo Indian. I boiled the possibilities down in the who-do-I-know-what-do-I-know kettle, and what remained was my Navajo friend.

Her name was Dolly Roberson, and she was married to John Wayne's stunt man, who was also a great friend of ours. Dolly had grown up in Monument Valley watching John Ford's film crews make movies. Her uncles had been in Ford's Westerns ever since he had directed *Stagecoach* in 1939. Their faces had grown older over the years, but they were still recognizable. They played the parts of Apaches and Cheyennes. They played good Indians and bad Indians.

I had heard all the stories about these special men and had howled with laughter at some of Dolly's memories. Yes. This was good stuff. Worthy of the interest of even *American West*. There was nothing remotely like it in any of their past issues, so I decided to give it a try and write a query letter.

It was six weeks before I heard from Mae Reid-Bills, the Managing Editor. Her response was cool and cautious. A definite *maybe*: "We might possibly be interested in looking at an outline."

Just an outline. Only an outline. The bare bones of an idea, nothing more. But it was a foot in the door. Maybe is almost yes. It is more yes than it is no.

I dashed off a response, indicating that *American West* would have my outline by the end of the week. Then I called Dolly and took her to lunch, where I heard again some of the wonderful stories about *The Stanley Boys*. That night I worked on the outline, perfected the lead until it fit *American West* style, and had it in the mail the next day, along with another enthusiastic cover letter.

Whew. I wiped my brow, flaunted Mae Reid-Bills' letter in front of my friend, and then waited. And waited . . . and waited.

Eight weeks later I received my second *maybe* letter. *Maybe* they *might* want to see an article "on-spec."

"On-spec" means that you must go ahead and write the article, getting it near perfect before it is submitted, and then the publisher still has the right to say, "No, thank you very much." "On-spec" is risky only for the writer— that is, you spend time working on something with no guarantee that anyone will want to publish it—and is often a necessary part of breaking in with a new publication.

Needless to say, I was ecstatic! They wanted to *see* my work! At this point I called Editor Bills. Was there a special slant they might like added to the material? How many words? How soon would they like it completed? We set a two-week deadline.

After I hung up, I wrote a follow-up letter confirming everything we had just talked about and telling the editor how much I looked forward to working with her on the project. The ice was just beginning to thaw. It was the ice that protects all editors who spend their time answering the queries of flakeball-would-be-writers who never follow through. (I would not like to be an editor. They put up with so much nonsense and yet are still required to be polite!)

I finished the first draft early. A cover letter accompanied it, expressing my hope that the concept was all there, but that I was willing to continue to work on the story if the editor saw any weak areas.

Once more I waited.

Eight weeks later I got my precious manuscript back with a list of editorial changes they wanted me to make. This meant that the entire story had to be rewritten.

Was I unhappy? I will admit that it entered my mind that this was a tough process. Then I made another phone call to discuss concepts and wrote another letter, which repeated what we had talked about and my promise to have the changes made in two weeks.

This whole process was repeated once again. Waiting. Rewrite. Submission. Waiting. And then came the magic letter! Maybe had turned into a *yes!*

One full year after my friend's challenge, I held a copy of *American West* in my hand—with my article in it. Beside my name was the name of the friend who said it couldn't be done receiving coauthor credit! I think I sent Mae Reid-Bills flowers that day! I was really proud of being published in *American West*.

I continued to submit ideas to them, and the next few stories I wrote for them required hardly any rewrite at all. I gained a whole new set of friends, and I eventually placed the *American West* logo on my credits right next to John Wayne Enterprises . . . but that's another story.

Selecting a Strong Idea

So you've found a publication that seems to have a lot in common with your background, knowledge, and interests. Now you have to decide what you are going to send them. But how do you select the best story idea to develop?

Your very first step should be to consult the Lord and seek His guidance. James 1:5 says: "If any of you lacks wisdom, he should ask God, who gives generously to all without finding fault, and it will be given to him."

Do you believe that God has called you to write? If so, would He create that desire in you, only to leave you floundering in confusion? Of course not! God has been developing your unique perspective through your life experiences, and you can rely on Him to lead you to very specific subjects to write about.

What does Proverbs 3:6 instruct? "In all your ways acknowledge him, and he will make your paths straight."

Don't think for even one moment that this refers only to hyper-spiritual things, or that God only concerns himself with using you to deliver critical, world-shaking insights. He is vitally interested in your development as His child. When your kids come to you with a crayon sketch of a horse that looks like a three-headed caterpillar, do you say, "Go away. And don't bother to show me your art unless you're ready to produce the Mona Lisa"? However modest your initial goals, however simple your first attempts, remember: The God who already formed your past also knows your future.

As an illustration of God's leadership and sovereign ability to use even the tiniest circumstances to direct our lives, let me tell you the following story.

Early in my career I wrote an article for *The Western Horseman* magazine entitled "Horse Colic and Your Horse's Diet." Hardly a piece loaded with enormous significance or enduring worth, wouldn't you agree? Yet because of that article and similar offerings over a period of time, I developed a real quality, working relationship with the editorial staff of that publication. This close partnership made them receptive to a later story idea I had about interviewing movie stunt men, specifically those involved in Westerns. During one of those interviews it was suggested that I might have overlooked a terrific possibility close to home. It seemed that John Wayne's stunt-double, a man by the name of Chuck Roberson, actually lived in my hometown.

I contacted Chuck, expecting nothing more than a few good stories and possibly another magazine article. But Chuck was a terrific interview! He had gotten into films in the 1940s and, besides doubling for Duke for thirty years, had doubled for Clark Gable and Robert Mitchum, among others. He had been in on the beginning of real movie stunt work: classic, breathtaking scenes done with live action, not speeded-up camera shots. He could tell stories all day long.

"Chuck, you really ought to write a book," I said. To which he replied, in his best aw-shucks cowboy manner, "I'd never get it done. Whyn't you do it?" This collaboration resulted in *The Fall Guy,* and Chuck's close relationship with John Wayne not only led Duke to write a foreword for the book, but also resulted in my going to work as a researcher and writer for Wayne's Batjac Productions. (This was also how I met Dolly, Chuck's wife, and her uncles, whom I talked about earlier in connection with the *American West* article.)

All from an article about horse feed.

Well, you get the idea. God had been directing my writing long before I could see where it was headed, and He cares about your writing too.

Back to the subject at hand: selecting a story idea. After you've consulted the Lord, your clippings file and magazine analysis can go to work for you.

Suppose that you have recently discovered an interest in scuba diving and have been reading up on the sport in *Skin Diver* magazine. You begin to wonder if you could write for that publication.

Reviewing your clippings folders reveals nothing under the headings of sports or hobbies, but a faint memory begins to surface. Then you remember, and in a very unlikely spot—the folder marked "Law Enforcement"—you find it. A reference to a specially trained unit maintained by your local sheriff's department to do underwater recovery of evidence. (Remember the scene in countless movies where the villain throws the murder weapon off the bridge?)

Into the back issues of *Skin Diver* you plunge to see if they have published such an article recently. Since the answer is no, you have a green light to consider the possibility further. An analysis of several issues throws some cold water (pun intended!) on your idea—the periodical seems to deal solely with recreational diving and travel. Then another angle comes to mind. In almost every issue there's a piece devoted to training (for example, how people learn to become hard-hat divers and where they go for instruction).

Now you've hit it. Some sport divers do, in fact, turn their hobby into a livelihood. Certainly they as readers, and therefore the publication, should be interested in hearing where they can obtain specialized education. Could you interview the local officers about the underwater recovery unit, developing a story favorable to law enforcement and of interest to those seeking a career in diving? (This idea sounds so good that I may want to pursue it myself!)

———————

Let's look at another example of how a story idea might develop. This time we'll start with the clippings file and work toward the magazine.

Suppose you come across a brief blurb in your local paper announcing that a Christian author whom you admire is going to be in your town for a book-signing party. You'd enjoy meeting her, so you make a note of the date and time and plan to attend. Then another thought crosses your mind: Could you arrange an interview with the author and develop it into a magazine article?

Of the publications you'd like to write for, which is likely to be interested in such an interview? *Virtue* seems a good possibility, and a quick glance into *Writer's Market* reveals that this magazine accepts interview/profile submissions between 600 and 1800 words in length. Their guiding statement points out that they "encourage women in their development as individuals and provide practical help for them as they minister to their families, churches and communities." Since our author has written several books to help career women balance those responsibilities with their families' needs, this match seems ideal.

What else must you consider at this point? Certainly you'd want to see if *Virtue* has already interviewed this particular author, and if so, how recently. A new article may be appropriate if a considerable time has elapsed since the last one, if the author has written something new and helpful since then, or if she has recently received some additional recognition.

Are there other possibilities? How about this one: *Writer's Market* notes that *Confident Living* is interested in "interviews regarding people in fundamental, evangelical Christian circles." Moreover, they advise contributors to "use illustrations of your own experiences or of someone else's when God solved a problem similar to the reader's." Does that sound familiar?

Or, how about a secular possibility? You happen to know that the visiting author has an extremely large and devoted local readership. In fact, this individual's work is so popular in your community that several self-help groups regularly use her books as resource material. Do you think that such a community phenomenon might be interesting to a local or regional publication? What do you know? *Writer's Market* reports that your community's lifestyle magazine accepts articles that are "upbeat and of demonstrable local interest."

Now, because this is a "religious" author, you may have to "sell" the secular editor on the idea, but if you believe that you are in touch with the concerns of your community, what better place to try?

――――――

Let's work through one more example of the process of connecting a story idea with a potential publisher. This time you have an idea about a topic that is of vital concern to you personally, but which did not come from your clippings file or a periodical of interest. You have been avidly following the increasing demands for freedom and democratization in Eastern Europe. National news broadcasts devote nightly coverage to the subject, and newspaper headlines announce each new wave of protest and achievement. But nowhere have you seen any coverage of the reaction of Eastern Europe's long-suppressed churches. Has the church leadership played an active role in the changes, or have they been hanging back? Does the trumpeting of newfound freedom also herald a return to freedom of worship or a return to biblical values and beliefs?

A brief visit to your church library produces the names of a few missionary organizations serving Eastern Europe. Phone calls to their headquarters yields this answer: "Yes, we know about the activities of Christians behind the Iron Curtain and their reactions to the current happenings. Yes, we can arrange for you to speak with one of our officers who has recently returned from a visit to Eastern Europe."

Might some Christian publications be interested in such a story? Since your efforts could possibly mean increased publicity for the missionary organization, do you think they'll be cooperative? In both cases the answer is yes.

By looking for personal, human-interest anecdotes, you might even capture national attention. At the other extreme, you certainly would be able to interest a denominational publication with news geared to their particular readership.

Exercises

1. Select the newspaper clipping that interests you most. Focus on a specific aspect of it and decide what slant you should take and which publication you should contact.

2. Select the publication for which you would most like to write. Go through all your folders, examining each clipping, until you find the story idea you believe will have the greatest appeal to its readership.

*B*ut everything should be done in a fitting and orderly way.

1 Corinthians 14:40

*T*he art of acceptance is the art of making someone who has just done you a small favor wish that he had done you a greater one.

Russell Lynes

Chapter:

12.

Me (Query) Contact an Editor (Query)

We had just moved to the mountains, and I settled into our new home with relief. I had resolved to do consultation work on only a very few scripts. Unless the life of a loved one depended on it, I would never drive on a Los Angeles freeway again!

I varnished the wood ceiling. I baked bread. I picked elderberries and made jelly. I even wrote a few stories about the horsemen in our hills and sold them to magazines.

That was a mistake. Word got out that I was a writer. A real, living, breathing, *published* writer! Then somebody heard I'd worked for John Wayne. No one was quite sure what I had done, but I had written "something" for "the Duke," and people now stared at me in the local cafe. Then I overheard two women in the little general store discussing how snooty I was! How I really thought I was hot stuff!

The truth was that I was self-conscious. Nobody likes to be stared at while eating a hamburger in a cafe. Also, I didn't see anything particularly glamorous or unusual about being a writer. I had spent so many years writing full time in an office with other writers that I simply thought of writing as a job, a profession, a vocation, like any other. Writers were people who went to work every day like everyone else.

The comment in the general store really hurt. I just wanted to be one of the mountain folks. I wanted to be accepted and invited to brandings because they liked me, not because I could write about them.

So I worked hard at my new image. I hung wallpaper. Painted. Bought a plunger for the toilet. When I went to the store, I tried extra hard to be friendly. I didn't want to look or talk or act like a writer—whatever that meant.

"Hi there! How ya doin'? Got any Liquid Plummer? We sure should have had the septic tank pumped before escrow closed! Yup! No one is real sure where the septic tank is! . . . Oh? You know someone with a backhoe? Can I have his name and number?"

I had just called the backhoe man and the pumping service when I heard a timid knock on the door. It was not the knock of a backhoe operator or a septic-tank pumper.

I opened the door in my best *"Well, howdy!"* manner. Before me stood a young woman in bell-bottoms with a child on each hip. She looked lost, shaking back her long, straight, sixties-style hair.

"Hi," she said so softly I could barely hear her. "Are you *the writer?*"

I could not deny it.

She said hello again and told me her name . . . "and I want to be a writer," she concluded.

I felt like asking her why. Instead, I said, "How nice," and invited her in. I thought she might be the mayor's daughter or something, and I could not bear the thought of more talk about my snootiness making the rounds. She looked tired from lugging the kids, so I said, "Would you like to sit down?"

She did, and the kids jettisoned from her hips with squeals of delight. They ran into our son's bedroom to color on the new wallpaper.

At that very moment the septic-tank man and the backhoe both rumbled up the drive. I excused myself and went outside for thirty minutes to discuss the logistics of the operation. When I returned, my guest was still on the couch and the bedroom had interesting new murals. I longed for the freeways of Los Angeles again.

"Well, so you wanna be a writer?" I asked through gritted teeth, and sat down.

"Yes. I live back on the forty acres. We don't have electricity . . . no phone or anything . . . or I would have called you first. I really feel that the Lord is leading me to be a writer, and when I heard that you are a Christian and you teach at the college and you wrote for John Wayne . . ."

Did they tell you my mother's maiden name? I wanted to ask. *Weren't you afraid to come to the house of such a snooty person? Weren't you afraid I would pull the ears off your children when they colored on my wallpaper?*

I stifled my Hollywood cynicism. "Are you taking any writing classes?" I asked as the backhoe began grinding and whining.

She had to speak up to be heard over the noise. "Correspondence . . . children's writing."

I knew of the course. Three hundred dollars for tuition, and the results were seldom of any benefit. But there was something so hopeful in her voice that I didn't have the heart to say what I was thinking.

"Have you been published?" I asked.

"I sent some stories in two months ago."

"Articles?"

"Children's stories."

The aroma in the air indicated that the backhoe had struck gold, but my guest did not seem to notice. I longed for my air-conditioned office on Wilshire Boulevard where the air was tainted only by smog and cigarette smoke. Where everyone was already a writer.

"Let's go get a glass of iced tea at the cafe," I suggested, preferring the stares over the smell.

I grabbed a piece of paper and my current copy of *Writer's Market* while she cornered the children and reattached them to her hips.

The cafe was cool. The children were turned loose in the parking lot to chase two old dogs that liked to bark at stock trailers. The iced tea had no unpleasant aftertaste. And I sat facing the wall so people could not watch me drink.

I figured if I sat here long enough and was helpful enough, I would be able to return home alone and my toilet would flush again.

"What magazine did you send your stories to?" I asked.

She gave me the names and I found them in the *Writer's Market*. Their blurbs indicated that the magazines did not take unsolicited manuscripts.

"Did you send a query letter to the editor?"

"What's that?" she asked in true blank innocence.

"That's a letter you send to the editor of a magazine in which you tell him or her what a great idea you have and how you would like to know if the magazine would like to see it on spec—"

"What does *on spec* mean?"

"That means on speculation . . . to see if the magazine would like to publish your article."

"Why not just send them the story?"

"Because it is important to ask. That way, if they say 'Yes we would like to see your story and see if you can write,' they will be expecting your material to arrive and it won't get lost in the slush pile. They want to see it."

Between more glasses of tea we reviewed the qualities of a proper query letter:

1. Short and to the point.

2. Displays enthusiasm for the magazine and the possible project.

3. Includes polite and complimentary statements about the publication.

4. Hopes for a positive response and the opportunity to write for the publication.

5. Requests further writer's guidelines.

6. Encloses an SASE (Self-Addressed, Stamped Envelope) for mailing reply and writer's guidelines.

7. *Important point!!!* All correspondence to a magazine editor should be neatly typed on your own professional stationery! Stationery should give your name, address, phone number, and any published credits you think might help establish your credibility. If you have no credits, then place the title "Free-lance Writer" after your name.

When I mentioned the importance of professional stationery, the young woman looked disappointed. She did not have the money for such an item. I explained that an attorney or a business person would not consider sending a letter on plain typing paper. She needed to dig deep and find the amount for that small investment.

The final point on my list also added to her unhappiness.

8. Do not approach a publication with fiction! Start with a nonfiction article idea.

In fifteen minutes I had shot down all the young woman's hopes of becoming an instant success as a Christian children's author.

"Then what am I supposed to write about?" she asked,

her chin quivering with disappointment.

"Why not write about something children are doing? Something that a child you know has achieved to the glory of the Lord! Do you know any kids like that?"

Indeed she did. She knew two wonderful high school girls who served the Lord by teaching handicapped children to ride horses. She knew another who raised state champion lambs for 4–H. As she told me these stories, she became more and more excited.

"Great!" I said. "Now let's go back to my place and do something to get you started."

Some publications accept phone queries in lieu of letters, and one of her chosen magazines happened to fall in that category. This was perfect! I suggested that she find a sitter immediately and then return to my house.

By the time the septic-tank crew departed, the young hopeful was coming back up the road alone.

When we sat down together at my dining room table with the phone, she was trembling. Had she forgotten how to dial a phone or was the prospect of talking to an editor frightening her? She had not been shy about coming to my door, so I assumed it was the telephone that made her nervous.

I presented her with copies of two of the work sheets I use in my classes, "Contacting an Editor With a Story Idea" and "Tips to Remember When Phoning an Editor." While I scrubbed the crayon off my son's bedroom walls, she studied the work sheets and filled in the blanks.

———

My young visitor's story has a happy ending. Sitting at my dining room table that afternoon, using my phone, she contacted an editor and received a positive response to her phone query.

She left my home with these instructions:

Go home and immediately write a follow-up letter telling the editor:

1. It was great to speak with you about my article idea.
2. I will have it on your desk in _____ weeks.
3. I am looking forward to working with you.
4. If you have any additional ideas on the story, please give me a call.

Since the young woman did not have a telephone, she gave my number to her newfound editorial contact. She also went to a quick-print company that very day and had her own stationery made up.

Today she is a well-known and successful free-lance writer. (This is a TRUE STORY!)

Exercise

1. Complete a "Contacting an Editor" work sheet.
2. Make the phone call!

Contacting an Editor With a Story Idea

Publication:..

Name of Editor:...

Telephone:...

Address:..

....

....

Number of words per article:..

Number of free-lance articles accepted per issue:..................

....

Number of articles overall:...

....

Topics (indicate style of story: interview, human interest; hard lead
   news or soft lead):..

....

....

....

....

....

Payment:...

....

Kill fee:...

My Story Ideas:

A...

....

....

B...

....

....

C...

....

....

Important Tips to Remember When Contacting an Editor with Your Story Ideas!

1. Editors are people too! You may be calling on a day when the Editorial Department is desperate for a good idea! Relax, and remember—they need you as badly as you need them. Be friendly and confident.

2. Make certain you are familiar with the publication! Read several back issues and be ready to comment on and *compliment* such things as content and layout.

3. Check your *Writer's Market* for the editor's name, then check again on the masthead of the most recent issue of the magazine to be certain that editor is still with the publication.

4. Chances are that a secretary will direct your call to a junior member of the editorial staff. If this happens, be friendly and positive and remember to *write down that person's name!* Direct your following correspondence to that editor. Remember, today's Assistant Editor or Editorial Secretary may be tomorrow's Managing Editor!

5. Be enthusiastic in presenting your story idea! Let the editor get a sense of your excitement for the project.

6. If the editor is simply not interested in that subject, then have your list of additional topics on hand so you can suggest alternatives.

Ask the Right Questions

7. In contacting a publication for the first time, always extend the courtesy of offering to let them consider the work "on spec." This means that they are not obligated to publish, but that they will definitely be taking a look at you as a professional writer.

    If the editor agrees to see your work "on spec," ask a few questions that will involve him or her in your creative process:

    a. "I was thinking of doing the piece as an interview, similar to the article in last month's issue by _____ . Does that sound as if it might work? Or would you prefer another approach?"

    b. "I noticed you used two color photos and three black and white in _____ article. Would you like me to submit all color transparencies with the story?"

You get the point. Have a list of intelligent questions that relate to articles in previous publications and INVOLVE THE EDITOR!

*I*t is better not to vow than to make a vow and not fulfill it.

Ecclesiastes 5:5

*T*ell everybody that you live in one hotel and live in another. When they locate you in the other move to the country. When they locate you in the country move somewhere else. Work every day till you're so pooped that about all the exercise you can face is reading the papers.

Ernest Hemingway

Don't Be a Deadbeat!

Redman survived the winter in the high pasture, and months of exercise through the numbing cold of the snows brought down the swelling in his leg completely. The vet examined him and explained that while he must never race again, he would in time make a fine saddle horse.

From the beginning, Redman had been trained to race, but there was no room for the high-strung temperament of a thoroughbred on the mountain trails. So our daughter Rachel began retraining Redman as a saddle horse.

Day after day, week after week, she worked patiently with him until he was at least passable on the trails. But he was still not *sensible.*

One afternoon he fought Rachel as she worked to make him cross a small creek at the bottom of our hill. Frightened, he spun and reared slightly, then spun again, refusing to cross. Rachel was handling the situation very well, but the sight of such a small girl arguing with such a large horse made me uncomfortable. So I took over.

Mounting Redman, I rode him to the top of the hill, then reined him back down for a fresh approach to the

119

creek. I had neglected to let down the stirrups of Rachel's saddle, and they were inches too short for me. As Redman neared the creek, he stumbled and brought his head down and to the side. The rein slackened as I leaned forward with his motion, and then the worst happened . . .

As my left leg pushed the stirrup forward, the rein suddenly caught beneath it! Redman jerked his head up as he tried to regain his balance, but the snagged rein pulled his head to the side. He fought against it. The forward momentum of his stumble now became an uncontrolled tumble toward the creek. I jumped from his back, trying to get out of the path of his fall. I landed on my feet below him to the left. He reared and fell backward.

The last thing I remember is seeing twelve hundred pounds of horseflesh rolling over the top of me . . .

I was lucky. When I woke up, only my leg and foot were broken. The horse was fine.

This story has no moral. I could not figure out how to make a lesson for writers out of *never-ride-short-stirrups-downhill-on-a-green-broke-horse!* However, there is a valuable lesson in what followed!

There I was, encased in plaster from hip to toe. By the time I felt like writing again I had missed four important deadlines with major magazines. Too defeated to reschedule the missed interviews, grouchy and miserable, I sat around for weeks until I was able to manage crutches.

All the editors were sympathetic and understanding. Maybe it helped that I sent each of them a snapshot of me in my cast beside the contented and oblivious horse, vowing that the next two horses I named would be *Miss Deadline* and *No Income!*

Everyone was laughing but me!

Circumstances beyond a writer's control are certainly justifiable cause for a missed deadline. Death is one acceptable excuse. It should be your own, however. Illness is a maybe. Injury is also a maybe—provided you have a horse to blame.

The point is, to make it as a writer you must establish yourself as a paragon of dependability. If an editor wants your article on Friday, you'd better have it finished Wednesday night and in the Express Mail-Overnight Delivery envelope on Thursday. Flood, fire, famine, emotional distress—none of these matter a hill of beans to the editor with a magazine to get out. If you cannot meet your deadline, have someone on hand with a camera to get a picture of you laid out in your casket, because that is exactly how the editor will picture you!

If you have established yourself as a reliable and consistent writer over a period of several years, or if you have a long-standing relationship with an editor, you may get away with a missed deadline once or twice. But woe to the novice who contacts an editor with a story idea and then fails to follow through! Any further communication from you will be read with a sneer and placed into the basket marked "Flakeball!"

A deadly enemy roams about writers' conferences seeking hopeful writers to devour. The polite name for this enemy is *procrastination*. Scripture calls it LAZINESS!

Check out your concordance. Proverbs 12:27 says: "The lazy man does not roast his game." Have you been out hunting for stories? Maybe bagged a few good ideas, and then never done anything with them?

Proverbs 26:15 teaches us that "the sluggard buries his hand in the dish; he is too lazy to bring it back to his mouth." Have you ever presented a story idea to a publisher and then failed to follow through? Opportunity is placed on a table before you, but unless you take advantage of it, it will rot away before your eyes.

Every writer must have "hand-mouth coordination." In order to succeed, you must be willing to make your hands do what your mouth promises.

Proverbs 26:13 offers a clear look at one motivation for procrastination: "The sluggard says, 'There is a lion in the road, a fierce lion is roaming in the streets!' "

Ah, yes. You can always find a reason not to write. Maybe you are afraid of failing. Maybe you are tired. (We won't even go into what Proverbs says about sleeping versus working.) Maybe your child has the mumps. Maybe you had an argument with your spouse. Maybe a horse fell on your leg . . .

Whatever name you may give to your Procrastination Lion, I guarantee that the beast will devour you and all your hopes if you lead it around by a leash.

"See," you say to yourself, "this is my lion. Every time I sit down to write, he growls at me. I just have to feed him a few more days and then he will go away."

Unfortunately, the lions who hang around writers will serve you up as the main course.

With that in mind, it is now time to *put the lion to sleep!*

Before you read further, get out pencil and paper and list all the *lions* in your life—all the things that somehow keep you from writing. Then ask yourself one question, honestly, before your Lord about each: "Is this a valid reason, or is it an excuse?"

Can you commit these things to the Lord along with your hopes and dreams as a writer?

———

Christians who write for the paid consumption of others bear a great responsibility, as we have already discussed. Being directed by God to be His voice is an undertaking that demands scrupulous honesty and absolute accuracy.

A Christian writer's responsibility is not confined to a careful handling of the written word however. Christians must be markedly honest and fair in their business dealings so they do not bring shame on the name of Jesus. This means that the author who professes Christianity must honor contractual obligations with utmost integrity.

Nowhere is this more evident than in the matter of deadlines. If you agree to produce a document by a given date, then you do everything within your power to meet that commitment. This may mean long hours, sleepless nights, and the delay of some other pleasurable pastimes.

You must understand that publishing production schedules involve many people besides you. Time must be allowed for editing, data entry or typesetting, and the actual printing. Any publisher, Christian or secular, becomes irritated, to say the least, when schedules have to be juggled because the writer's part of the process is delayed.

A flagrant disregard of this minimum courtesy will happen only once: you won't get a second opportunity. Frequently asking for extensions of deadlines is just as bad and soon leads to a reputation for being unreliable.

How much better it would be if you as a Christian writer were always more prompt than the rest of the writers in the world! This means presenting your manuscript on time and in an acceptable form. It means providing the necessary photographs and illustrations, properly captioned and labeled, with the submitted article and not "to follow later." It means responding to editorial suggestions promptly and politely.

All of these statements about meeting your obligations undoubtedly seem obvious and unnecessary. Unfortunately, the obvious is often overlooked or ignored. That's why many great ideas never find their way into print. It's easier to get excited about writing a query letter and celebrating a favorable nod from a publisher than it is to actually sit down and produce a finished piece of work. Satan loves to use the normal interruptions of daily life to delay and hinder Christians from doing something of importance to the kingdom of God.

Don't let him get away with it! Keep your vows and deliver your work on time.

*H*e who answers before listening—that is his folly and his shame.

Proverbs 18:13

*L*earn how to conduct an interview. Whatever form of nonfiction you write, it will come alive in proportion to the number of "quotes" you can weave into it naturally as you go along. Often, in fact, you will find yourself embarking on an article so apparently lifeless— the history of an institution, perhaps, or some local issues such as storm sewers—that you will quail at the prospect of keeping your readers, or even yourself, awake. Take heart. You will find the solution if you look for the human element. . . . Somewhere behind every storm sewer is a politician whose future hangs on getting it installed and a widow who has always lived on the block and is outraged that some . . . fool legislator thinks it will wash away. Find these people to tell your story and it won't be drab.

William Zinsser

Chapter:

14.

Interviewing Unmasked

She was a dear Christian friend, and I knew she wanted to be a writer. But in all the years I had known her, she had never taken advantage of the fact that I might be able to open some doors for her. So on her birthday one year I asked her two questions: "What celebrity would you like to meet this year?" and "What magazine would you like to be published in?"

In answer to the first question, she immediately named a well-known Christian singer. I will call the singer *Sue Mee,* (which she might do if I used her real name!).

In answer to the second question, she blurted, "I would love to be published with *Saturday Evening Post!*"

That afternoon we phoned an editor I knew at the *Saturday Evening Post* and asked if he would be interested in an "on-spec" story about "Sue Mee at home." He said sure. Why shouldn't he want to see a story on-spec? After all, he didn't have to buy it.

The second order of business was to phone the Actors Guild in Hollywood and find out the name and address and phone number of Sue Mee's agent. This was also a simple matter.

The next stage could prove more difficult. Setting up an interview through an agent or press agent is not always easy, but it's the only way to go (unless you know the celebrity personally, and even then sometimes it's necessary). Agents are bombarded by phone calls and letters from flakes who want to meet the stars. Therefore, they will insist that you write a letter explaining your exact purpose for wanting an interview and naming your editorial contact at the publication for which you are writing.

We phoned the agent and then immediately wrote the required letter stating purpose and requesting a *press kit*.

The *press kit* is a folder containing photographs of the celebrity, a biography, and other promotional materials. Often the photographs are of better quality than anything you could take yourself, and the biography and other materials will help you in composing questions to ask during the interview.

Happily, we had no difficulty in setting up our interview with Sue Mee.

The day before the interview we drove to Los Angeles. (Yes, I actually returned to the L.A. freeways for this one!) We stayed where I had stayed for years, at the Holiday Inn on freeway 405, which was only minutes from Sue Mee's home.

Now the story gets interesting . . .

You see, my friend had brought her entire wardrobe with her because she could not decide what to wear. So I was awakened at six in the morning to find her trying on each item in turn, even though the interview was not scheduled until eleven!

"How do I look?"

"Is this okay?"

"What do you think about this sweater?"

Before long I was ready to toss the suitcase out the

window along with my friend. I'd forgotten how much I hated hotel rooms and getting up before the sun.

"Well, actually, she won't care what you wear as long as you look professional and businesslike," I tried to reassure my friend. "Why don't you wear one of those four suits? I promise you, she's just a person—like you. She might even be nervous about meeting us. So relax!"

My friend did not relax. On the way to breakfast, wearing one of the suits, she tripped on some stairs and tore the *one pair of pantyhose* she had brought! Disaster. The Holiday Inn on 405 did not have even one pair of pantyhose in the gift shop. I drove to a store I knew of. When I returned, my friend had changed into a different outfit and was redoing her makeup.

"You need to calm down," I said, noticing that her lips were shaking weirdly.

"That's easy for you to say! You met John Wayne!"

"Well, he was just a regular guy too. I'm telling you, these people are just people!"

After she had donned new pantyhose and a different suit—a blue one to match her freshly applied eye shadow—we got into the car and drove down Sunset Boulevard. My friend gawked and chattered like the tourists who follow the Star Maps through Beverly Hills. I told her if she didn't calm down, the deal was off. I would call and cancel the interview and tell the *Post* it hadn't worked out.

Instantly she became contrite and silent. Her lips still trembled, but when we turned off Sunset onto a side street and parked in front of Sue Mee's nice but rather ordinary home, my friend smiled and sighed with relief. Had she expected a palace?

The porch light was on, and two empty water bottles sat on the front step. There was a station wagon in the driveway. It looked like a regular house where real people lived.

At the stroke of eleven we knocked on the door. Silence. No one answered. A full minute passed. I knocked again. More silence. Another full minute. This time I rang the doorbell *and* knocked. Had we made a mistake? Wrong day? Wrong time? Wrong house?

My friend grew calm and pale with disappointment. "What do we do?" she asked.

"Go to lunch and call?" I suggested.

We knocked one more time, and then we heard it! Ahha! Inside the silent house the shrill, happy squeal of a small child! The squeal sounded again in reply to our elated knock!

The door opened two inches. At doorknob level appeared the face of a woman who was hiding behind the door! Her hair looked as if it had been charged with electricity! Dark mascara circled her eyes and ran down her cheeks. *Who was this masked woman?*

"May I help you?" she croaked.

"Uh . . . my name is Bodie Thoene . . . and uh . . . we're with *Saturday Evening Post*. We have an appointment at eleven with—"

Suddenly the door flew back. "Oh NO! Oh! I *forgot!* Oh, come in!" It was Sue Mee herself, standing there in her husband's red pajamas. She had been asleep. Suffering with morning sickness, she had simply been asleep!

I tried not to look at the disheveled celebrity whose face was as red as her pajamas. She looked . . . like people with morning sickness look who just wake up. Yes, she was a mess. Just like anybody in those circumstances would be.

While I was being polite and trying not to look and trying to reassure Sue Mee that we could come back another time and that it really was okay . . . my friend was gawking with a wide smile on her face. Running mascara and oversized red pajamas had put her at ease!

Our gracious and embarrassed hostess urged us to stay. While she ran down the hall to pull herself together, we watched *Dumbo* (one of my favorite movies) on the VCR with the delightful squealing child who had betrayed his sleeping mother.

Sue Mee did her best to recapture her dignity, but I don't think she looked either of us in the eye the entire hour. The interview was punctuated by her toddler's insistent interruptions.

The piece for *Saturday Evening Post* ended up being very small and very memorable. And my dear friend never again trembled at the thought of meeting *anyone*!

Interviews are unique and individual and unpredictable because people are unique and individual and unpredictable. So there are no set rules I can give you. Just a few hints.

1. If possible, research other articles that have been written about the person you are going to interview. Often you will find that other writers have left out points you would like to see expanded. What hasn't been covered in the other articles? What else would you like to know about this person?

2. Write out a list of questions. Include topics from the *5 Ws and the H*. Having the list in hand will help you if the conversation drags.

3. If you happen to get a person who really loves to talk, don't let your prepared list break up the flow of conversation.

4. Make sure your tape recorder works before you get there.

5. Take extra tapes and batteries. Just in case.

6. If you are going to need photographs, let the interviewee know that and take along a good camera. If you are not adept at photography, by all means find someone who is. If you do, however, be sure to notify your subject that a photographer will be coming with you.

7. Always end your interviews by asking your interviewees what they would like to say if they could tell the world anything at all, or some variation of that question. Usually this gets you some real humdinger answers.

8. Dress appropriately. Nothing gaudy. A business suit is a good choice in most situations—unless you're covering a horse race!

9. If you are a woman, always bring an extra pair of pantyhose!

All hard work brings a profit.

Proverbs 14:23

The profession of writing makes horse racing seem like a solid, stable business.

John Steinbeck

Loving a Many-Slanted Thing

So there I was on crutches. Smitten hip and thigh and still encased in plaster, I had come to the mountains surrounding Lake Tahoe to cover a horse race known as the Tevis Cup. The race would be run over one hundred miles of tough, inhospitable mountains, from Squaw Valley to Auburn, California. One Horse. One rider. One hundred miles in only twenty-four hours!

I had originally contracted to cover the race on horseback, but now I had to be content to cast longing looks at the 350 riders and their super-fit mounts. A dozen other press people wandered around the campgrounds; their tape recorders, cameras, and bewildered looks gave them away. The place was a confusion of horse trailers, vets, horses, crews, and spectators. The ground was pocked with holes and horse droppings, making it nearly impossible for a writer on crutches to navigate.

I looked at Brock in despair. "I'll never make it. I might as well call the magazine right now and tell them—"

"Kill the lion," he grinned.

So I swallowed hard and hopped toward a vet who was checking the respirations of a horse. *They shall know thee by thy stethoscope,* I thought, watching him work. Then I whispered to an observer, "Do you know the name of the vet?"

Indeed, the cowboy knew. Armed with this information I approached the doctor. "My name is Bodie Thoene. I'm a writer with—"

"What happened to you?" He eyed my crutches.

"A horse fell on me," I answered.

Now he eyed me with respect. I was not just another journalist; I was a horsewoman! The other writers and photographers wore designer jeans and boots that had barely touched the ground. But there I was with horse manure on the end of my crutches and a little story of my own to tell! Yes. He was happy to talk to me. Then he introduced me to the top riders in the race.

Brock snapped photographs while I filled reels and reels on my tape recorder. Somebody brought lawn chairs and a feed bucket for me to prop my leg on. I was in heaven. I had material enough for a dozen stories and the race hadn't even begun!

This was the sort of problem we writers dream of. Too *much* material! More than I could use, unless I wrote a book about the Tevis Cup. I would not need to do extra research or spend hours expanding on the stuff I had. One horse to one rider. One hundred miles in one day. And only one article for one magazine!

Where should I draw the line? What one angle should I settle on? Should I approach the editor with an idea for expanding the Tevis Cup into several articles in the same issue? That was my first choice.

After compiling a list of possible stories, I contacted my editor and asked him to choose one. He was uncertain, so I asked if he might be willing to publish three or four stories in the issue. He considered the idea for a day and then got back to me. No, one story would do it. And could I get it to him on Friday?

Since he was one of the editors I had failed when Redman landed on me, I had the article on his desk three days early.

Which left me with a vast collection of wonderful details begging to be used. Looking over my list of topics again, I wondered whether any of them could be tailored to fit the magazines I wrote for on a regular basis. One was a well-known women's publication, another was an American history journal, and the third was another equine publication.

Carefully choosing the subjects that might strike a chord with each editor, I spent a few minutes on the phone and ended the morning with assignments "on spec" for three additional articles for each of these publications.

There is a lesson here for every free-lance writer: Stretch your information. Stretch your possibilities. Multiply your dollars!

What can you do with one horse race, you ask? What can you do with one topic that interests you? Read through the following lead paragraphs of the articles I wrote from the Tevis Cup material.

Women's Magazine

Each year, the quiet aftermath of the famed Tevis Cup Endurance ride is a clutter of individual stories. What-ifs, almosts, might-have-beens and I-should-haves crowd against the fact of what-is and who-won. It is all these factors that make a horse race. Although conditioning, great skill and horsemanship may form a wide chasm between the first-place rider and the last weary finisher, often only chance and a few ticks of the second hand separate first place from the others in the top-ten riders.

Marjorie Pryor, winner of the Tevis Cup last year, returned to the rugged Sierras with her 13-year-old Arabian horse in hopes of capturing the cup once again.

American History Journal

Nearly one hundred years have passed since an enthusiastic young journalist named Edward Sanguinetti mounted an Arabian horse for the first time. His praise for the breed, recorded in *Harper's New Monthly Magazine,* stirred the imaginations of two young men who were considering the advice of Horace Greeley to *"Go West, Young Man!"*

Equine Magazine Number One

Dr. Todd Nelson, DVM, chief veterinarian for the 100-mile Tevis Cup endurance race, looked out over Squaw Valley. The valley floor was teeming with lean, ready horses and contestants. "No horse people," he said quietly, "know more about their horses than endurance people."

Equine Magazine Number Two

For Todd Nelson, DVM, chief veterinarian for the staff of fifteen monitoring the Tevis Cup race, the event means three days and nights of long hours and hard work. "Before, during, and after the ride," he says, "a horse is probably checked more times than an average horse is checked in a lifetime."

All four of these articles take a different tack. Each fits the style of the respective magazine and offers a totally different emphasis.

Multiple story angles is one way to conserve your energy and add to your income.

Exercise

Review your strongest story idea. Try to imagine three *additional* approaches in the presentation and development of the facts.

*T*he more the words, the less the meaning, and how does that profit anyone?

Ecclesiastes 6:11

*L*ike most writers, I don't like to write;
I like to have written.

William Zinsser

*W*hat is written without effort is in
general read without pleasure.

Samuel Johnson

Editing Till It Hurts

*O*nce I complete an article or a chapter of a novel, the really hard work begins.

First, Brock reads back every word I have written. Then we discuss the strengths and weaknesses of the material. I have to admit that this can be painful at times, but he is almost always right in his assessment.

Often I have to leave the manuscript and go vacuum the carpet to let off steam. (Usually the vacuum cleaner is a couple of feet off the floor. It makes a lot of noise so I don't have to!)

When I return, I am ready to rewrite the material. And it is inevitable that there will have to be a rewrite. That is a fact of life for a writer.

Beginning writers almost never believe that good writing is rewriting. They think if they attend enough seminars, sign up for enough workshops, read enough self-help writing books, and *think* enough, when they sit down to write, all the words flowing onto paper or into the word processor will be golden. Worse yet, they believe those words are inviolate; and woe to anyone who suggests that something could be improved!

Now this may sound extreme and unreasonable, and it is meant to be; but there is an element of truth present. Writing so seldom comes easily that once an author has achieved something bearing the appearance of a final product, it seems thoughtless, even cruel, to suggest that it should be revised.

But remember, revising serves one purpose: to make your writing readily accessible to the reader.

Readers should not have to struggle to follow the development of your story or reread passages to see what you are driving at. And they should feel satisfied with both the content and the treatment of the subject when they are done.

Consider this analogy: A hungry diner sits down in a carefully selected restaurant to eat a delicious meal. The diner is paying for, and has every right to expect, a meal that is tasty and well prepared. He expects the courses to be presented in an orderly fashion—dessert doesn't come first nor soup last. While he may be willing to try the unknown, sample a new recipe, he does not want to have to pick too many fine bones out of the fish nor eat with dirty table service. At the conclusion of the meal he should be able to say that the individual dishes were enjoyable and that the entire meal was satisfactory. A good restaurateur knows that if a diner goes away unhappy, he will not soon return. And readers will not be loyal to an author who disappoints or displeases them.

With that in mind, here are some practical guidelines for the revision process.

First of all, *find someone reliable* who can read the first draft of your article carefully and critically and point out any weak areas. You may even want to ask more than one trustworthy person to read your work. Then two or three days later, with their comments in hand, reread the article and begin to revise, looking carefully at the following specific areas.

Word Choice

This does not mean we're going to spend time discussing the need for proper spelling. Either get a typewriter that beeps at errors or a helpful spouse, friend, or someone who is paid to catch spelling mistakes.

By word choice we mean selecting the most appropriate word or words for your intended purpose. For instance, "obsolete" is more effective and much more considerate of your reader's attention than "old, outdated, and in need of replacing with a newer model." Also, make sure that the word you choose is correct; for example, don't use "credulous" if you mean "credible."

Don't use slang words like "awesome" or "gross." These are perfectly legitimate words but have been so overused and misapplied that they are best avoided. Also, be cautious about using jargon. "Ram" and "rom" will be acceptable in a magazine dedicated to computer devotees, even if unexplained, and "redeemed" and "justified" within material directed to a completely Christian readership, but not to a wider circle.

Don't try to overpower your readers with your vocabulary. "The sentient being was senescent" may sound eloquent, but no reader wants to have to stop every two lines and look up a word in the dictionary. By the same token, don't try to be too folksy or cute.

Finally, beware of overusing a word or an expression. Rereading a paragraph that appeared correct when first written may reveal that you used the word "transported" three times. Two of these could be replaced with "carried" and "moved."

Your thesaurus and dictionary should become well worn during this part of the process.

Sentence Structure

Make it as easy as possible for your reader to understand what you are saying. Shorter sentences are almost always better than long, convoluted ones.

Correct punctuation is a must. Sentences cannot be read correctly nor thoughts conveyed accurately if the punctuation does not support the intent. Attention-getting punctuation such as parentheses and exclamation points are sometimes appropriate, but use them sparingly; otherwise they either lose their effectiveness or become distracting.

Awkwardly constructed sentences distort the meaning, sometimes with humorous results. Take the sentence, "I was shopping for antiques the other day when leaving the store I saw a most amazing clock." Get the idea? Unfortunately, this unintended humor is very distracting, and a reader's attention is too valuable and too difficult to recapture to let it slip away because of careless writing.

Sentences can also be destroyed, or their effectiveness reduced, by the overuse of modifiers. To avoid sounding dogmatic, writers will sometimes lard their work with unnecessary qualifying words such as "somewhat" and "many times." These can turn a straightforward comment like "People who have smoked for many years have difficulty quitting" into a cumbersome one like "Many times people who have smoked for many years have somewhat of a difficult time quitting."

The careful writer also avoids run-on sentences. If a particular phrase just has to be included, consider substituting it for another or making it a part of another sentence.

As an example, look at this sentence produced by a writing student after an interview exercise: "Chuck Roberson is a fine-looking man, despite his leading a rough-and-tumble life full of danger and excitement, and it is remarkably satisfying to hear him tell it." Whew! There's enough material there for two or three sentences at least.

Finally, watch for common grammatical mistakes in the areas of subject-verb agreement, tense, and plural formation. Easily remedied flubs like "they was" or "in the old days cars are" grate so badly on a reader's ear that they bring thought progression to a screeching halt.

Content

It is always better to show than to tell, and someone else's anecdote quoted by you is much more effective than trying to put it in your own words. Anecdotes, quotes, and statistics are the stuff of which credibility is made, so review your work to see that you have adequately used these to satisfy and convince the reader. Do not rely on merely presenting your opinions.

Resist the temptation to editorialize. If you are trying to emphasize a point or point of view, do it with the words of those whom the reader will acknowledge to be experts entitled to have opinions worth reading.

Above all, see that your revision ties up loose ends and answers all the questions you have raised. This is a fine distinction but an important one. If an issue is not within the scope of your article, it is better not to raise it at all than to mention it and not adequately address it. If readers have their own questions after reading your work, fine; you have interested them in wanting to know more. But you dare not bring up a question within the context of the article and then ignore it or leave it unanswered. Such

145

treatment not only leaves the reader unsatisfied but is as rude as not replying to a question directed to you.

Example: "There are three keys to developing your memory. The first is to concentrate. The second is to prepare a mental outline, and the third I forget."

You may groan, but this is how your reader feels when you leave loose ends or unanswered questions. You do *not* want the reader to have a sense of something left undone at the conclusion of your article.

Style

Stylistic considerations fall into two categories. The first is your personal style or voice. This quality will develop with time and experience, and it is what will cause a core of loyal readers to eagerly anticipate your work. Personal style may be as markedly associated with the author as William Buckley's vocabulary or Bill Cosby's folksy humor. Both men have devoted readers, although their styles vary dramatically, and both have earned the right to have an identifiable style.

More important to the developing writer is the second category: the stylistic concerns of the publication to which you are submitting your work. We have already reviewed the importance of studying and trying to match a magazine's style, so this is just a reminder. Check your completed piece for conformity to that style—length, vocabulary level, paragraph length, and so forth. This is as important as checking the punctuation and spelling. It is also the area where the editor who likes your concept and its development will be most helpful in sharpening the end result. A good editor is concerned with style, tone, and pace, and will seek to tighten and sharpen your prose.

*M*an looks at the outward appearance.

1 Samuel 16:7

*F*or the novice free-lance writer, the editor's office may seem like an inner sanctum. . . . But you'll be closer to reality—and closer to getting inside the office—if you imagine the following: a typewriter and possibly a word processor on a little table; mismatched chairs crowded around a gray metal desk, with calendars, memos, and page layouts taped on plaster walls; through the venetian blinds, a view of a parking lot. On the littered desk, alongside an overflowing in-box, are a salad in a plastic container and a mug of cold coffee. The editor's office, in short, is usually about as glamorous as that of a free-lance writer.

Patricia Tompkins

*N*o manuscript should bring more clutter to an editor's already cluttered life.

Carol Johnson

Chapter:

17.

Dressing for Success

*T*hree questions I am frequently asked when I speak are: "How do I send my material to a publisher?", "What if somebody steals my idea?" and "If somebody buys my story, can I ever publish it again?"

Packaging Your Manuscript

Mailing your article is like going on a job interview: The more presentable and tastefully dressed you are, the greater the likelihood of return interviews and long-term relationships.

To dress a manuscript for success includes the following:

1. Have a clean copy of the manuscript with a title page and blank endsheets.

2. Place your name and the title of the article at the top of every page of copy.

3. Enclose the manuscript in a clear plastic folder with a slip-on plastic spine. Don't use staples, paper clips or three-hole punches.

4. Insert the plastic-bound manuscript in a plain blue

or buff folder with two inside pockets. Place your cover letter and manuscript in the right-hand pocket, with the cover letter in front; any photographs or illustrations should go in the left-hand pocket. The latter should be protected by individual clear-plastic, pocketed sheets, so they can all be laid out to view at once. On the back of each photo put your name, the title of the article, and the caption material. (Identify the 5 Ws on each photo and let the editor decide what to include.)

While publications can generally work with prints, ask if they prefer transparencies (slides). If this is the case, then provide a separate list of captions, matching each transparency to its caption with a stick-on number.

ALWAYS keep a clean copy of your article for your own files. NEVER SEND OUT YOUR ONLY COPY OF ANYTHING!

You should also take a simple step to protect yourself against piracy. Mail a third copy to yourself by certified mail, and when you receive it, leave it sealed. Should a question of copyright violation ever come up, the sealed and dated envelope will confirm your authorship as of a specific date.

You should also mail your completed manuscript package by certified mail with a request for a return receipt. This practice will not only notify you that your work has been received by the proper person but will also demonstrate to the editor that you value your own efforts.

Know Your Copyrights

I had been publishing regularly for a number of years before I encountered my first pirate. That one experience made me mop my brow in relief and thank God for the copyright law.

The article I had written was a well-researched piece including interviews with movie directors, major film stars, and behind-the-scenes crew members of MGM/UA. From start to finish the piece had taken me four months to complete. Long-distance phone calls, travel expenses, and precious time had made the project costly for me. After we deducted all the expenses, there was little profit in the venture, but the work had given me the unmeasurable reward of great satisfaction.

The story appeared in a major national magazine, and as soon as the issue hit the newsstand, congratulatory phone calls poured in. Three additional assignments were garnered from that one story.

Four months passed and new work absorbed me. The MGM story was filed away and almost forgotten, along with other old assignments.

I was on my way to cover the remake of *Stagecoach* when I spotted my story on the front page of a tabloid in the airport news rack.

At first I couldn't believe it! My story . . . my own story . . . four months of my life! My lead paragraph! The exact words from interviews I had battled to obtain! Transitions and descriptions and . . . and . . . *someone else's name on the piece!* "Walter *who?*"

The sheer brazenness of this theft was astonishing, but it was this last insult that galled me to the core. I had written under a dozen pseudonyms, but *this was not one of them!*

I found a telephone and called Brock. Brock called our attorney. Only our attorney was calm. He smiled over the telephone.

"Not a big deal," he said. "The man is a thief as surely as if he robbed a bank! Violation of copyright is a crime. No problem. We'll get you what you deserve."

The lawyer was true to his word. The publisher who had stolen my work paid dearly for the article he had stolen. Brock and I paid our happy attorney and had just enough left over for a piece of pie and a cup of coffee. Frankly, I felt I deserved more than pie and coffee, but, as Brock pointed out, that was not the point! The thief had gotten what *he* deserved!

After all the years of writing and faithfully copyrighting my material, I finally understood the reason behind it!

Protecting Yourself Against Piracy

Some beginning writers believe that copyrighting a work is a complicated process. Nothing could be further from the truth. Copyright law protects your rights to duplicate, sell, and market your creation from the moment it's completed. All that you need to do is note your name, the date completed, and the word copyright (or the copyright symbol ©) on your work (e.g. , © 1990 by Bodie and Brock Thoene). This simple step guarantees you and your heirs the exclusive right to market your material for your lifetime plus an additional fifty years.

A manuscript or collected group of manuscripts may be registered with the Copyright Office by obtaining a form from the Register of Copyrights, Library of Congress, Washington, D.C. 20559. Ask for the Copyright Information Kit. This action is not essential, but does provide some additional legal protection in the event of piracy. For instance, you cannot collect for court costs or attorney's fees in the event of a lawsuit on a previously unregistered work, and a suit for damages as a result of piracy cannot be brought on an unregistered piece.

In any event, you should take the additional step suggested earlier of sending a certified copy of your work back to yourself and leaving it unopened.

Remember that ideas and research material in the form of facts and statistics as well as titles cannot be copyrighted. Good ideas can be and are stolen, so this probably explains why active authors discuss their published works freely, but are reluctant to go into detail about writing that is contemplated or in progress.

What Am I Actually Selling?

Magazines and other periodicals typically buy first serial rights. This allows the publication the right to issue the article for the first time only, reserving any further rights to the author. These reserved rights include the right to sell the article for reprinting, the right to sell the work for collection in book form, and the right to market the piece for television or other adaptations.

From an author's point of view, the more limited the rights sold, the better. Selling only the First North American Serial Rights, for example, means the writer has the right to market the work outside the U.S. and Canada.

Some publishers may ask for "all rights," which means that after you have accepted their offer, the article is no longer yours to distribute or develop in any way. Be wary of granting such all-encompassing rights, particularly if you feel the material has additional potential.

Some periodicals will respond to a submission with a written contract, but many will indicate by letter that cashing their check confirms the author's acceptance of the terms contained in the letter. Sometimes those terms may be in fine print on the check itself, so be careful what you sign or cash!

Avoiding Misunderstanding

Most publishers are scrupulously honest in the matter of authors' rights. Something that appears to be piracy is sometimes just an unfortunate lack of communication.

Most of these problems can be avoided by spelling out clearly in your cover letter exactly what rights you are offering to sell, and by indicating whether you are simultaneously submitting your work elsewhere. The *Writer's Market* entries for some publications will tell you what rights they buy and whether they accept simultaneous submissions. If this is not clearly spelled out, ask.

Of making many books there is no end.

Ecclesiastes 12:12

For several days after my first book was published I carried it about in my pocket, and took surreptitious peeps at it to make sure the ink had not faded.

Sir James M. Barrie

The important thing for a writer to remember about a book proposal is that it is essentially a selling tool. It is what determines if the publisher will buy the book and for what price.

Bill Adler

18.

Practically Perfect Book Proposals

Brock had remarked several times that books dealing with Christian financial advice seemed to fall into two categories: either they focused on families already in a credit crunch, or they were aimed at high-income families who were ready for estate planning.

"Nowhere is there a book for the 80% who are in the middle," he said. "These families are getting by, but they don't know about protecting their incomes or planning for retirement."

I let him get by with this remark about three times, and then I nailed him. "Why don't you write it, then?" After nine years in the financial business, Brock was certainly knowledgeable about the subject. And besides that, he could write.

You see, writing nonfiction is a matter of being able to communicate clearly. Knowledge is important, of course, but careful research can fill up gaps in expertise. What there is no substitute for, what research cannot provide, is clarity and *readability*.

Brock spent six months writing and revising, and the result was a highly readable and on-target book on family finances, *Protecting Your Income and Your Family's Future*. It is a good example of how nonfiction should be written: clear advice given briefly, backed up with true stories and cemented with practical, personal application.

Great books come from great ideas. Not all great ideas become books, however. That's because IT'S EASIER TO PLAY WITH AN IDEA THAN IT IS TO PUT IT DOWN ON PAPER. Just thinking about writing a book-length manuscript can be pretty overwhelming.

If you are considering writing a book, you need to do several things before beginning to write and before contacting a publisher.

First of all, do some market research. This means that you make a thorough examination of current books on the same or related subjects. You are not looking just to see if there are already published works, because undoubtedly there are, but to determine whether your work fills a "niche" or a particular unaddressed need. Compile a list of the books you find, together with brief comments about the emphasis of each and how the book fails to fill the need you have seen. Pay special attention to popular authors or works considered to be the best or most hopeful.

If, after this examination, you still believe your idea would add important information on a subject, or would present information better or in a new way, then you should write a "statement of need." For this, try to obtain quotations and other evidence to support your notion that your concern is shared by others. For instance, a quick survey of Christian psychologists reinforced Brock's belief that almost all marital complaints have something to do with money management.

Reduce to one typed page the most compelling reasons

why your subject needs to be explored and why your treatment of that issue will exactly fill the need.

Next, prepare a chapter outline. This need not be in extraordinary detail, but should reveal the major structure of the book. If each chapter will spring from a central idea, quote, or statistic, be sure to indicate it. Above all, show a logical development in your outline, giving the publisher an unclouded view of the progression of your thinking. You want them to be nodding in agreement as you raise and then respond to various points.

Think of each chapter as a magazine article. Your reader should be able to finish one chapter in one sitting and come away with a clear grasp of one main idea and a few practical applications. Showing through story and example is always better than telling; allowing the reader to respond to questions and exercises is better than lecturing. Keep it short and keep it simple.

Your sample chapter need not be the first chapter of the work, but it should be representative of your theme, style, and treatment.

When you package your material for submission to a publisher, include the sample chapter, chapter outline, statement of need, and market survey. You should also send a brief biographical sketch, emphasizing the background and education that have prepared you to write the proposed book. Be sure to include an enthusiastic cover letter indicating your belief in the importance and timeliness of the topic and your reasons for submitting to that particular publishing house. Convey your interest in working with them to make your project a reality.

Remember, you get only one chance to make a first impression, so be certain that your presentation is crystal clean and attractive. Determine beforehand the name of the acquisitions editor and direct your proposal directly to his or her attention. Mail the proposal by certified mail with a return receipt requested.

If you are fortunate enough to have more than one company interested in your work, give consideration to several factors besides just the amount of the advance, if there is one. How will your book be distributed? (That means, how will the publisher sell it and get it into book-stores.) Is there an advertising budget? Will the company aggressively promote your work?

Finally, be prepared to wait. *Writer's Market* says that the review process for a book manuscript takes from one to three months. The reality is that book projects may take one or two years from concept to published book. So don't get discouraged! Stay upbeat and enthusiastic!

*T*rust in the Lord and do good; dwell in the land and enjoy safe pasture. Delight yourself in the Lord and he will give you the desires of your heart.

Psalm 37:3–4

*O*ur admiration of fine writing will always be in proportion to its real difficulty and its apparent ease.

Charles Caleb Colton

Thoene and Thoene

You may have noticed that the names of two authors are listed on the cover of this book. Brock and Bodie Thoene. Husband and wife writing team. Thoene and Thoene. That's us.

You may also have noticed that the stories beginning several of the chapters are written in the first-person-singular "I." That's Bodie. She gets to do all the fun stuff. The technical information in the chapters—the really important stuff—is written by Brock and supplemented by Bodie in a dovetail process that meshes paragraphs and concepts together into cohesive subjects.

It is amazing, even to us, that it works as well as it does. More about that later . . .

You may be asking, "Since there are two writers on the project, why don't they write it in the first-person-plural "we" instead of "I"? Good question. Happily, there is a simple answer.

Just for a moment, imagine yourself entering the throne room of an ancient queen. Wrinkled and shrunken, the old woman sits on her throne and stares down at you through her pince-nez as you approach. Her mouth is twisted in a scornful smile. You are uncertain of protocol, so you stop and bow.

"Hello, Your Royal Majesty."

Her scowl deepens. "Are you addressing *us?*" she asks in a high squeaky voice.

There is only one old lady on the throne, so you figure she must be schizophrenic or senile.

"I am addressing *you,*" you explain.

"*We* are never addressed as *you,*" she replies haughtily.

"Well, I should hope not. I am me and you are you. It would be terrible if someone thought you were *me.*"

She blinks in amazement. You think you are getting through to her.

She speaks again. "How did you ever get into *our* throne room?"

There is still no one else in the room, so you ask, "Does this belong to somebody else too?"

"Indeed not! This is *our* royal throne room! Belonging to no one but the royal person herself! We demand that you leave *us* immediately!" Her face is red with rage. She looks as if she might have a stroke.

"Are you okay? You want me to call a doctor for both of you?"

"LEAVE US!" she shouts. "Guards! Expunge this person from our royal presence!"

Get the picture? In team writing the "royal we" can be a royal pain, leaving your reader feeling more than a bit uncomfortable, not to mention *confused.*

On the other hand, if we had written *"Bodie does this and Brock says that,"* the double perspective would muddle up the personal feel of speaking writer to writer, one on one.

Some articles do lend themselves to the use of the "royal we"; for instance, a "how-to" piece about the way you and your spouse remodeled your attic. However, usually when you are called on to write in the familiar, easygoing, first-person perspective, you and your co-writer will want to use the singular term "I."

———————

Brock and I have been working together since the first months of our marriage.

Organization and research are his main areas of responsibility. He builds the structure of plot line on which I hang the words. Before I begin to write each day, we pore over the research and the character motivation and the goal of every small section. While I write, Brock gives instant feedback as he reads the material to me and directs the flow of words and emotion into the proper channels. By the time a manuscript is completed, Brock has been over each page many more times than I have. Somehow it seems to work.

I suppose that the success of our Zion Series and Saga of the Sierras is one example of how God can take two totally opposite personality types and forge them into a team. If you had known us as kids, you would consider it a miracle!

Brock and I have known each other since we were three. Maybe longer, but that is as far back as we remember. We never got along. He was stuffy and intelligent. Straight *A* student. I was the class clown . . . and you've already heard about my grades.

When Brock would raise his hand to speak in class, I would make a face at my girlfriend. I called him "Encyclopedia Britannica," which I later shortened to *"Brockanica."*

He recalls that whenever I spoke out in class I usually ended up sitting in the corner. Sad but true.

While I was learning to write, Brock was learning to research and compile and structure vast amounts of information. What I could not do well, he performed with meticulous attention to detail. What he could not do . . . spin yarns . . . I became quite competent at. I became known as "The girl with the most creative excuses for cutting class." (If Brock wanted to miss class, he simply submitted a request to the teacher and it was granted.)

Our senior year in high school I noticed that he was handsome, and he happened to have a thing about red-haired girls, so we went out. Suddenly we discovered that we *liked* each other! He could talk about anything . . . a welcome relief from the dumb-jock types I had been dating. He discovered that I could hold my own with him in a political discussion. (It was the era of Vietnam and we went round and round.)

My father liked Brock. My mother had become a Christian and began to pray that I might marry someone *so-o-o-o-o wonderful!* Two years later, after a stint covering the anti-war demonstrations in San Francisco, we were married.

I packed up my typewriter and moved to Baylor University in Waco, Texas. The partnership began there.

Baylor University has one of the finest library collections of original works by another writing team, Robert Browning and Elizabeth Barrett Browning of *"How Do I Love Thee?"* fame. In the library there is a bronze casting of their hands. Robert's hand is large and strong. Elizabeth's is small and delicate. Standing before that small memorial of their love, my new husband took my hand in his and said, "Just think. They spent a lifetime together—working together and loving each other. We can do that. Just like they did."

God must have heard that whispered desire of our hearts. The forging of our two opposite personalities has not always been easy, but the result is so much fun for us! In every case the load of writing is cut in half. (There are also some wonderful personal benefits, of course, but this book is not about that.)

The Successful Writing Team

If you feel that God is leading you to work with a co-writer, here are some guidelines from Thoene and Thoene:

1. Spend time in prayer for the person you are working with.

2. Divide the responsibilities. One person writes so many chapters while the other takes on a different aspect of the project. One provides the research while the other writes.

3. Only one member of the team should talk to editors and write query letters!

4. Find constructive ways to praise your partner's work. If you have a criticism, don't just gripe; gently suggest *what* might be done to improve the work.

5. Talk about items you disagree on over lunch or dinner in a public place. That way you will not be tempted to smack your co-writer in the nose or throw your typewriter at him!

6. Learn to laugh.

7. Learn to give in. Remember, you need the different perspective that your co-writer lends to the task of writing.

Your Partnership

Whether you find yourself with a co-writer or not, you do have a Partner, the best of all partners. He never gives bad advice, and He always meets His obligations. He provides the inspiration and you provide the perspiration.

Jesus wants you to excel as you serve Him with your writing, and He will give you all the experiences and opportunities you need to both prove and improve your skill.

The promise Brock and I constantly rely on is Psalm 37:3–4: "Trust in the Lord and do good; dwell in the land and enjoy safe pasture. Delight yourself in the Lord and he will give you the desires of your heart."

"You mean that's it?" you may be asking. "That's all there is to writing for publication?"

Yes. That really *is* it! Boil it all down, and the mystery of writing for publication amounts to this:

Trust in the Lord . . .

Do good . . .

Doing good means learning the basic principles found in a little book like this. It is the harness and yoke that will help you pull the load *as far as you want to pull it!* (Perhaps even all the way to a best-selling novel.)

DO GOOD . . .

Appendix

The Professional Free-lancer's Checklist

1. At the top of the list is your copy of *Writer's Market!* It must be the current issue so the material you glean from this precious volume is accurate!
2. Nearly every publication you will write for will have its own list of *Writer's Guidelines.* Send a self-addressed, stamped envelope to the magazine and request a copy of these guidelines. This will sum up the editorial requirements and needs of the publication.
3. The importance of appearing professional cannot be overstressed! When writing your query letters and follow-up correspondence to editors, make certain that you have your own *letterhead stationery!* Your *log, publishing credits,* and *emblems of professional writer's guilds* will help lend you credibility where it counts.
4. Public relations professionals understand the importance of a polished appearance when submitting a story for publication. Most writers submit material in a *press kit.* The *press kit* is a folder with two inside pockets. One side contains photographs and the other holds the story. When submitting your story for consideration, consider the first impression it will give when it is taken out of the mailing envelope. Will photos spill out onto the editor's desk? Are the pages of the story loose and easily lost or mixed up?
5. Inside your story folder, two items will help the editors remember who you are. A short one-paragraph *bio sheet* tells them just enough to demonstrate that you are a serious professional! Your *business card* can be placed in a file for future reference.

Biographical Information

Name . . . .
Education . . . .
. . . .
. . . .
. . . .
. . . .

Published in . . . .
. . . .
. . . .
. . . .
. . . .

Professional Organizations . . . .
. . . .
. . . .
. . . .
. . . .

Family, Interesting Facts . . . .
. . . .
. . . .
. . . .
. . . .
. . . .

Contacting an Editor With a Story Idea

Publication:...

Name of Editor:...

Telephone: ....

Address:...

....

....

Number of words per article: ....

Number of free-lance articles accepted per issue:.....................

....

Number of articles overall:...

....

Topics (indicate style of story: interview, human interest; hard lead
    news or soft lead):...

....

....

....

....

....

Payment:...

....

Kill fee: ....

My Story Ideas:

A. ....

....

....

B. ....

....

....

C. ....

....

....

Important Tips to Remember When Contacting an Editor with Your Story Ideas!

1. Editors are people too! You may be calling on a day when the Editorial Department is desperate for a good idea! Relax, and remember—they need you as badly as you need them. Be friendly and confident.

2. Make certain you are familiar with the publication! Read several back issues and be ready to comment on and *compliment* such things as content and layout.

3. Check your *Writer's Market* for the editor's name, then check again on the masthead of the most recent issue of the magazine to be certain that editor is still with the publication.

4. Chances are that a secretary will direct your call to a junior member of the editorial staff. If this happens, be friendly and positive and remember to *write down that person's name*! Direct your following correspondence to that editor. Remember, today's Assistant Editor or Editorial Secretary may be tomorrow's Managing Editor!

5. Be enthusiastic in presenting your story idea! Let the editor get a sense of your excitement for the project.

6. If the editor is simply not interested in that subject, then have your list of additional topics on hand so you can suggest alternatives.

Ask the Right Questions

7. In contacting a publication for the first time, always extend the courtesy of offering to let them consider the work "on spec." This means that they are not obligated to publish, but that they will definitely be taking a look at you as a professional writer.

   If the editor agrees to see your work "on spec," ask a few questions that will involve him or her in your creative process:

   a. "I was thinking of doing the piece as an interview, similar to the article in last month's issue by _____ . Does that sound as if it might work? Or would you prefer another approach?"

   b. "I noticed you used two color photos and three black and white in _____ article. Would you like me to submit all color transparencies with the story?"

You get the point. Have a list of intelligent questions that relate to articles in previous publications and INVOLVE THE EDITOR!